the series on school reform

| Patricia A. Wasley | Ann Lieberman | Jose‸ |
| University of Washington | NCREST | New York University |

SERIES EDITORS

(Continued)

the series on school reform, *continued*

At the Heart of Teaching

A GUIDE TO REFLECTIVE PRACTICE

GRACE HALL MCENTEE

JON APPLEBY ♥ JOANNE DOWD

JAN GRANT ♥ SIMON HOLE ♥ PEGGY SILVA

with Joseph W. Check

Foreword by Mike Rose

Teachers College
Columbia University
New York and London

The "Tuning Protocol", "Consultancy Protocol", "Critical Incidents Protocol", "Guided Individual Reflection Protocol", and "Fishbowl Protocol" were developed as part of the Coalition of Essential Schools' National Re:Learning Faculty Program and further adapted and revised as part of the work by Annenberg Institute's National School Reform Faculty Project.

The "I Remember" protocol and the "Peer Editing Protocol" were developed by the Boston Writing Project and the National Writing Project and are reprinted in this volume by permission.

Published by Teachers College Press, 1234 Amsterdam Avenue, New York, NY 10027

Library of Congress Cataloging-in-Publication Data

At the heart of teaching : a guide to reflective practice / Grace Hall McEntee
. . . [et al.]; foreword by Mike Rose.
    p. cm. — (The series on school reform)
  Includes bibliographical references and index.
    ISBN 0-8077-4349-6 (alk. paper) — ISBN 0-8077-4348-8 (pbk. : alk. paper)
      1. Effective teaching.   2. Teacher effectiveness.   3. Reflection
(Philosophy)   4. School management and organization.   I. McEntee,
Grace Hall.   II. Series.
  LB1025.3 .A87 2003
  371.102—dc21   2002040924

ISBN 0-8077-4348-8 (paper)
ISBN 0-8077-4349-6 (cloth)

Printed on acid-free paper
Manufactured in the United States of America

10 09 08 07 06 05 04 03   8 7 6 5 4 3 2 1

To Ted Sizer
and to all the students and teachers
from whom we have learned.

Contents

Foreword

A few years ago, I participated with some of the contributors to this book in a writing workshop. As I look back through the notebook I used that day—filled with sketches, questions, stretches of give-and-take among the participants—I'm struck by a brief event that occurred about half-way through the workshop. The facilitator was asking us to create some images of classroom life, and from those images to generate ideas about teaching. I flipped to a fresh page of my notebook—I'm looking once again at it now—and wrote a word or two . . . that I then scratched out. Blank. Blank page. We were in the ballroom of an old hotel. I could hear a faint piano through the vents. I took a note on that. Overhead, on the frieze that framed the ceiling, stylized cherubs were caught in motion, knees bent, arms raised. I scribbled something about them. The other participants seemed to be doing O.K. All the people I've taught, all the classrooms I've visited, and I'm unable to come up with one vivid image!?

I just can't write well—if at all—from a distance. It's hard, as I was finding out yet again on that day, for me to conjure, away from the classroom, a sharp recollection, a thought worthy of expression. I need people and things: a student paper, a photograph, my hurried sketch of the way desks are arranged. A sound, even, or a smell: the dissonant notes of band practice or a sniff of acrylics. I don't want to make too much of this quirk of the way I write, but it got me to appreciate the value of particulars, of the importance of talking and thinking about schools from the stuff of classroom life. This surely is one reason educational policy so often seems to miss the mark, to not strike at the core of a problem. It is developed in the abstract.

The authors of this book write from the moment, out of the lives of the young people they teach. And they have, over the long haul and with the support of others like themselves, developed an orientation toward their teaching that enables a reflection on the particulars of practice. In the ensuing pages they share this orientation—its evolution and its method—and help us get in close to the classroom. We are guided to go back over the tumbling rush of experience, to replay it, to puzzle over it, to slow things down. To slow things down enough to appreciate the graceful move, map it perhaps, but, also to wonder why in the world we chose *that* passage or said what we said to *that* particular kid. Such deliberation can enhance one's skill, but, in addition, can lead beyond one's own practice. In the chapters that follow, we see the examined classroom moment open up beyond itself: to reflection on habitual school routines and familiar structures; reflection on leadership and governance, on community, on funding and politics; and reflection on the way we define and organize knowledge and on the very purpose of mass education in a democratic society. As one of the teachers quoted in this book puts it:

> The difficulty in writing for me isn't to find stories to tell; teaching is a profession that generates stories. Instead, it is to create narratives and understand teaching in a larger sense, in the context of my life, my school, my community, and all the debates and issues surrounding education.

As you read through these chapters, you might well find yourself taking issue with particular observations and conclusions or with the very way a certain author is framing an issue. And you might wonder how you, in your situation, could possibly engage in this kind of reflection with this kind of support. These would be legitimate concerns, and the authors, I suspect, would be the first to admit their fallibility and their good fortune. But there is a broad message to the chapters as a whole, one beyond specific discontents. It is that teaching is a complex, ever-evolving activity, wrought from disciplinary knowledge, human encounter, and institutional negotiation, and that doing it well means thinking hard about it, weighing, deliberating, asking others for their take on your action. It means that what we do is rarely free of at least some ambiguity, some uncertainty, one solution chosen from several perfectly reasonable alternatives. It means that we sometimes nail it, do the right thing, foster the kind of intellectual and social growth we desire. And, it means that at other times we are less successful, OK maybe, muddle through, stumble terribly. But such is the nature of this remarkable, difficult, rewarding work. And, thus, it demands reflection.

What we are too often given instead to help us get better at our teaching is the half-day in-service, the two-step or five-step or whatever-step routine, the prepackaged script. Now, I'm all for a trick or two, a nifty technique; we need every little tool we can get. But teaching with art and conviction requires so much more. Typical professional development fare will rarely take us close to the particulars of our own practice, nor help us foster the reflective cast of mind so necessary to become a true agent in this complex profession. As I read through these chapters, finally, it's that sense of thoughtful becoming, that possibility of action in the midst of uncertainty that, at the end of the day, is the promise of this book.

—Mike Rose
UCLA Graduate School of Education
and Information Studies

Acknowledgments

We have lived these stories with many other people. Our writing represents the work of colleagues and mentors who have pushed our thinking and supported our growth. We are grateful to the following people and organizations:

The Coalition of Essential Schools, the National Re:Learning Faculty, the National School Reform Faculty, and the Annenberg Institute for School Reform who believe that teachers can transform education.

All the teachers who joined us at writing workshops over the past 10 years.

The writers whose personal writing experiences motivated and inspired us.

The students and teachers whose classroom experiences provided our stories.

Family members who provided professional expertise every single time we asked. Thank you, especially to Lenore Collins, Paul Dowd, and Kate DeGuise.

Susan Liddicoat and Amy Kline who encouraged us and strengthened our writing.

Ann Marshall, our Prudence Island editor, who read every single word over and over again, checked our punctuation, and formatted our manuscript, thereby streamlining and polishing our work.

The Prudence Island community who ferried us, fed us, entertained us, and welcomed us to their beautiful island.

Matt McEntee, who allowed us to invade his home several times each year.

Grace Hall McEntee, the one link to all the individuals and organizations listed above, who motivated us, nurtured us, and opened her home and heart to share her writing life.

Introduction

JOSEPH W. CHECK AND GRACE HALL MCENTEE

We did not set out to write a book. The six of us—Jan, Peggy, JoAnne, Simon, Jon, and Grace—teachers from Rhode Island, Massachusetts, New Hampshire, and Maine, were in the midst of trying to improve our individual teaching. We came together for the first time to write about our practice through a project suggested to Grace in 1994 by Ted Sizer, founder of the Coalition of Essential Schools at Brown University. And we have stayed together since then, to deepen our understanding of how a thoughtful revisiting of our experiences can help us to become better teachers. We are Educators Writing for Change.

We have met and talked over long weekends three or four times a year, worked with other teachers around the country, and coached one another through observation of each other's practice and through the stories we have shared, first orally, then in writing. We, teachers of elementary, high school, and university students, thought we knew what reflection was—a revisiting of an event in order to understand it better. And today we confirm: yes, that was—and still is—our starting point. Now, we know that we must go beyond that.

WHAT IS REFLECTIVE PRACTICE?

For us, reflective teaching is peeling back the layers of our own daily work, looking under the surface of our own teaching, making a conscious attempt to see our teaching selves as students see us, or as an observer in our classrooms would. It also means looking at the wider contexts that affect our teaching—issues of social justice, of school structure, of leadership.

The familiar image of Rodin's *The Thinker* places the individual alone in a thinking or meditative posture. While we felt awe, both individually and as a group, as we viewed a casting of Rodin's masterful work at the Rodin Museum in Philadelphia, it is his *The Burghers of Calais* that comes closer to what we now understand as reflection. Rodin's burghers stand together in a circle of overlapping postures, one frowning, one stoic and smooth of brow, one covering his face in despair, one looking inward, another outward. They are a small community, each revealing a different reaction to a single event. Together they exemplify the complexity of human experience.

A group of teachers might pose for such a sculpture in response to a school shooting or as a team in an initial attempt to understand a student who has come to them. But reflective practice goes beyond varying reactions to a single incident. Articulation—the saying out loud or the writing down for sharing—of such an incident and the exchange of ideas become the catalysts for individual and collaborative thinking and the construction of new knowledge.

Reflective teaching is the opposite of what high school teacher Margaret Metzger (1993) calls *playing school*:

> A script we all know. Students line up in desks, sit passively, raise hands occasionally, pass in homework, and watch the well-intentioned and exhausted teacher intone over the materials. . . . Playing school destroys education because the students are not using their minds. They do not engage in challenging intellectual work. . . . They learn intellectual passivity. (p. 14)

Conversely, reflective practitioners combat passivity, constantly attempting to use their minds and to engage students in the same difficult activity, to dive deeper into their teaching and its effects, rather than drifting on the surface of practice.

We do think chin on hand; we meditate to unclutter the mind. We do stand with others to share reactions. But we also must deliberately process what has happened—alone or together—using various tools at our disposal. We decided to write a book to share what we have learned through individual experiences and collaborative revisiting of incidents and events.

REFLECTIVE PRACTICE
AND THE EDUCATIONAL PROFESSION

Over time and in community, our Educators Writing for Change have reached the understanding of reflective practice described above. We are sure this understanding will continue to evolve, just as we are aware that our definition owes a great deal to the way others have used the term over the past 20 years.

In the early 1980s Donald Schön (1983) focused attention on a new kind of thinking that characterized professionals-in-action: architects, engineers, doctors, teachers, and others. He asked:

> What is the kind of knowing in which competent practitioners engage? How is professional knowing like and unlike the kinds of knowledge presented in academic textbooks, scientific papers, and learned journals? (p. viii)

Schön's initial raising of these questions launched an entire body of professional literature, not the least in education. Among these follow-up works was Schön's own *Educating the Reflective Practitioner* (1987), in which he pointed out that:

> The problems of real-world practice do not present themselves to practitioners as well-formed structures. Indeed, they tend not to present themselves as problems at all but as messy, indeterminate situations . . . A teacher of arithmetic, listening to a child's question, becomes aware of a kind of confusion and, at the same time, a kind of intuitive understanding, for which she has no readily available response. . . . The case is not "in the book." If she is to deal with it competently, she must do so by a kind of improvisation, inventing and testing in the situation strategies of her own devising. (pp. 4–5)

The links between this kind of thinking and the then emerging fields of teacher research and practitioner-driven professional development are obvious, and have continued to grow more significant. Anna E. Richert (1991), for example, argues that:

> To respond appropriately to the changing circumstances of their work, teachers must learn to learn from their changing experiences in schools. But learning from experience is difficult . . . teachers must have time to think about that experience. Having an experience does not constitute learning about it; having an experience and then thinking about it to make sense of it does. But schools are not organized with time for teachers to "make sense" of their experiences. (p. 113)

Richert's point—that if schools are to change for the better, they need to become places where teachers can be reflective—leads inevitably to the question of school culture and its effects on the individual teacher. School culture has been described as "the way we do things here . . . that almost indefinable feeling in a school that lets new students and teachers know what is important and how they are supposed to act" (Richardson, 1996, p. 1).

School culture, the surrounding, normative medium in which practice exists, can either inhibit or promote individual change. There is no doubt that in many schools today, the culture does little to promote reflection. Karen O'Connor of the Massachusetts Field Center for Teaching and Learning finds that:

> Teachers not only need time to reflect—but help in learning how to reflect. We are all so busy *doing* that we need someone to help us sit back and deconstruct our experiences so we can make sense of them. This does not come easy to a lot of teachers who are used to making quick responses (Conversation with Joseph Check, February 2001).

The narratives and protocols in this book provide ways to make sense of what we teachers do and to discover new possibilities of how we might learn and teach in the face of pressures from sometimes indifferent or hostile school cultures.

As an organizational framework for *Reflection: The Heart of Changing Practice,* we begin at the center—with students in the classroom. From our experience we suggest ways for teachers to build reflective practice with their students. Chapters 1, by JoAnne Dowd, 2, by Jan Grant, and 3, by Jon Appleby provide classroom-centered insights. In these chapters students learn processes to become the protagonists in their own learning.

From there we move outward to the relationships among adults both inside and outside our classrooms, those relationships that strongly affect the culture of our schools. In Chapter 4 Peggy Silva presents a scenario and a protocol for individual students, their parents, and teachers to talk together about the student's performance.

In order to know students and to teach them to process their own learning within the world around them, teachers need to nurture their own ability to reflect and to remain vulnerable within their community of colleagues. Simon Hole, in Chapter 5, shows what can happen when teachers come together to share the stories of their daily lives. Chapter

6, by Simon Hole and Grace Hall McEntee, offers a protocol for reflecting alone and a slightly different version of that protocol for reflecting with a group.

A number of chapters in the book refer to Critical Friends, small groups of educators that engage in collaborative study with the goal of improving student learning by changing their own teaching practice. Through the lens of high school teacher Peggy Silva, Chapter 7 describes the process of reflective practice with colleagues in a Critical Friends Group.

Other stakeholders must be part of the process. Chapters 8, by Simon Hole, 9, by Jan Grant, and 10, by JoAnne Dowd tell stories of parents, a university supervisor, and a district administrator and policymaker engaging in the process of reflection with others to improve the quality of classrooms and schools.

In Chapter 11, Grace Hall McEntee shares the process of bringing teachers together to reflect upon and write about practice.

The framework of this book is not meant to illustrate or suggest a necessary sequence of prescriptions to improve schools. Our intent is to inspire and to provide examples and techniques for promoting reflective practice. Knowing that the cultures, problems, and achievements in every school are diverse and complex, we hope that the reader will take from this text what makes most sense within the context of a particular classroom, professional relationship, school, or district.

REFERENCES

Metzger, M. (1993, June). Playing school or telling the truth? *Harvard Graduate School of Education Alumni Bulletin, 37*(3), 14–16.

Richardson, J. (1996, October). School culture: A key to improved student learning. *School Team Innovator.* Available from http://www.nsdc.org/library/innovator/innn10-96rich.html.

Richert, A. (1991). Using teacher cases for reflection and enhanced understanding. In A. Lieberman & L. Miller (Eds.), *Staff development for education in the '90s* (pp. 113–183). New York: Teachers College Press.

Schön, D. (1983). *The reflective practitioner.* San Francisco: Jossey-Bass.

Schön, D. (1987). *Educating the reflective practitioner.* San Francisco: Jossey-Bass.

CHAPTER 1

Changing the Blame Game

JoANNE DOWD

Every morning we dance the same dance. Kids shuffle in and take seats. I enter and check the roll. Nick does something dumb. I kick him out. Slam! The glass in the door rattles. The other boys shut down. Another day of class.

A substitute teacher's cataloging of my students' unspeakable behaviors convinced me that we had to change the rhythm. Out of desperation, I tried a strategy illustrated in this chapter. It worked for that moment. Later it evolved into a model that I have used over time and across groups.

In order to develop a community of reflective learners in my classroom, I've needed to learn how to be reflective myself. I've learned to "be still" with a problem and, as the Quakers say, "Let the truth rise." This truth, when it has risen, allows me to discover my "next steps"—changes I need to make in my practice so my students and I can move in the direction of interdependence and mutual learning.

I had been away at a conference. A substitute teacher covered my English class, a particularly difficult group of freshmen. Upon my return, I was distressed by the report he left on my desk. A teacher's nightmare. "The kids were completely out of control. People were throwing things. Someone tried to flush a young man's backpack down the toilet."

My senior intern was overwhelmed. She reported there was little she could do but sit by helplessly. "I had forgotten what it's like to want a substitute for class so that you can just act up and have fun," she wrote in her journal. "The guys are a lot more dominant today. Only one or two of them are actually reading, but the girls are."

A number of boys had been unruly from the beginning of the year. They communicated with each other by kicking and writing on one another with chalk. They expressed annoyance by throwing each other's book in the trash. One student threw a temper tantrum whenever he was displeased.

This English class had an unusual makeup—19 boys and 6 girls. Academically, the heterogeneous group represented our student population in rural Maine. Throughout the fall the class had been participating in a variety of activities and discussions about respect. I had felt we were making progress. My reaction to the substitute's report was anger. How could my students do this?

A NEW VIEWPOINT

I could have spent the rest of the year frustrated by my students. I could have endlessly analyzed why they had no social skills, dwelling on their low socioeconomic backgrounds. Or I could learn to accept my students and find ways to make progress. After much soul searching and reflection, I realized my only choice was to accept my students as they were.

Over the weekend, crunching through fallen leaves, I walked for hours in the crisp autumn air. At first my brain whirled with questions. What had I done wrong? Why were the students acting like this? How much of a factor was the gender imbalance in this class? Eventually, the October stillness settled me. By taking the time to remove myself from and reflect upon my situation, and by looking at it from different angles, I was more willing to change my practice to better meet the needs of my students. This time—this time of stillness—helped my students and me to find our way toward becoming a cohesive learning community.

During my walks that weekend, my thinking gradually shifted from viewing my students as a problem to viewing our situation as an opportunity to learn something new together. The falling leaves signaled a time for change. Just as the trees lost their leaves and bared their branches preparing for the long winter ahead, I realized we should do the same. We needed to get to the underlying issues if we were going to survive the long Maine winter together.

I knew that the move from eighth grade to ninth grade was a difficult transition for most students. Our freshmen were accustomed to having the junior high school principal read the school rules over the intercom every morning. My students hadn't spent much time learning about democratic practices or decision-making. Now, abruptly, they felt the pressure for learning and responsible behavior squarely on their shoulders. My walks reminded me that I couldn't just give them the tools. We had to create them together.

A NEW PROCESS FOR PROBLEM SOLVING

Silence greeted me when I returned to class on Monday. Students busied themselves by taking out notebooks, pens, and reading books. No one made eye contact with me. They quietly waited for the inevitable lecture and reprimand. Instead, based on my reflections of the past weekend, I had a partially formulated plan. I tried the strategy of surprise.

"Today," I announced, "we have an opportunity to solve a problem together." Turning my back, both to portray trust and to compose myself, I drew on the chalkboard a chart that I had created over the weekend (see Figure 1.1).

I asked the students to write for five minutes about what had happened on Friday and what contribution each had made to the situation. I told them, "You will need to share what you have written, so be prepared." The only rule I imposed on this sharing was that each student was to focus solely on what he or she had done. I wanted each student to begin the process of owning his or her behavior. Students would be asked to share what they had written, as would I, and together we would fill in the "problem" side of the chart, as we each read. Free writing was part of our daily routine. While I frequently used free writing as a tool for self-reflection, I had never used it in this way. I had an idea that we would use the "journal sharing" as a jumping off point to complete the "problem" half of the chart. Then together we would move over to the solution side. The students quieted down and began writing. I wrote along with them. Silence filled the room. The only sound was that of scratching pens on paper.

When I asked who would like to share, Nick, the class clown, eagerly volunteered. He had written a clever poem about how sunflower seeds and grapes were flying across the room. His sharing created an opportunity for several other students to express how

Figure 1.1
Problem-Solving Process

1. Draw a chart on the board that has two sides separated by a line down the middle. Across the top of the chart write a "problem statement" (in the chapter example, my problem statement was "Behavior with the substitute teacher").
2. Allow the students to write silently for approximately 5 minutes about the problem statement. Remind them that there is no "pass" option in this exercise.
3. Hear from each student. As the students speak, it is important that they only speak about their own role, and take ownership of anything that happened.
4. As students are speaking and as they start identifying the problem(s), begin completing the "problem" half of the chart, under the subheading "student contributions."
5. At some point in the sharing it is important to recognize the teacher role in the problem statement with a subheading "teacher contribution."
6. If necessary, add a third subheading "other factors" that may have contributed to the problem (in our case, it was the substitute teacher).
7. When everyone has a chance to share, including the teacher, the group will move over to the solution side of the chart.
8. Together, the group will brainstorm a solution.
9. It is important in the solution that there is a measurable, observable solution and that both teacher and students have a role in making it work.
10. Collectively set a time to go back and revisit the solution (a couple of weeks) to see how things are going and make any changes necessary to the solution.

"cool" it was that things were thrown. They even confirmed that, indeed, someone's backpack was flushed down the toilet in the girl's bathroom. I took a deep breath and glanced out the window. Watching several leaves drift gently to the ground, I strengthened my resolve. We needed to make a change.

I found it difficult to reserve judgment and not react, but having reflected and set out on this new path, I knew that if I fell into the trap of expressing my anger, my whole plan would fail. I held my tongue, reaching again for the stillness. I used my energy to write the students' comments on the chart on the board, finding a moment's respite in turning my back to the group. I chose only to speak when students pointed fingers at others. "What did *you* do?" I repeatedly asked. "Arthur will have a chance to talk about what Arthur did."

A Different Voice

While most of the boys had spoken, I had yet to hear from a girl. As I had forewarned, I called on all those remaining silent. As the girls shared their writings, we heard a different perspective. Some were angry at the boys' actions. They claimed they had tried to keep the group on task, but most of the boys were out of control. The small group of girls feared that the entire class would be punished severely for the actions of a few, as had happened in the past. This new process allowed female students to speak up safely. It elicited new voices that otherwise may never have emerged.

We continued the process, creating as we went, together filling the chart on the chalkboard. I had only the vaguest idea of where this might take us, but my faith in my students as well as the desperate need for solutions drove us forward. I asked the students to identify their contributions to the problem. They owned up immediately and, in some cases, proudly to their actions. I silently reminded myself to trust the process and told myself, "The truth will rise."

Moving over to the next column on the problem side of the chart, I asked how the substitute teacher and I had contributed to the problem. An awkward silence ensued. This was a question they were not used to being asked. Finally Megan read from her journal, "The substitute didn't even try to keep control of us. Once, when Arthur threw something across the room and hit another kid in the head, the substitute said, 'nice shot.' After a while, some junior football players stopped by to talk with him and he ignored us for the rest of the period."

I acknowledged that I could have left clearer instructions for the substitute teacher and could have worked with the front office to ensure the most appropriate substitute had been chosen for this particular group.

A Breakthrough

When we moved on to the solutions side of the chart, the students admitted that they could have been more helpful to the substitute by telling him about activities that are part of our classroom routine. Others vocalized that even if the substitute couldn't find my lesson plans, they could have used their time to study. Students recognized that they shouldn't have behaved any differently than they do when I'm present. They admitted that they broke our food rule (students may bring food and drink into the classroom as long as they don't leave a mess or throw things), and those involved with throwing food voluntarily gave up their food privileges for a week.

This discussion was a breakthrough. Unlike any lecture or reprimand I could have given, the problem-solving strategy forced students to confront their own behavior and create a solution. When I admitted I had a role in the problem and therefore would have a role in the solution, I had planted seeds for change in our classroom.

The establishment of a structure to talk about problems openly, without fear of retribution, made a difference. Students who once remained silent, particularly girls, began to speak up more often. "Louder is better" no longer remained the norm. The displeasure of peers carries more weight with students than does the displeasure of teachers.

At the end of the period, I reflected upon the success of my new structure. Jotting down as much of it as I could, the success of my seedling plan had evolved in response to the students. I had stumbled upon something that could be incorporated into my teacher's toolbox for future "bad days."

Part of my master plan for the year was to allow students to work with me to develop an aspect of the curriculum. I had intended to do this during the second half of the year, saving it for when my students would be ready. They were ready sooner than I expected.

I tried the problem-solving model once again when our class was bogged down in a brainstorming session. I was trying to brainstorm ideas with them for a unit and they were exhibiting some of their less than desirable behaviors. I put the problem-solving chart into use. Our consensus solution was that we would create a unit on public speaking and debate. Because of the success of the problem-solving strategy, I was more open to changing my practice yet again by being more receptive and responsive to the students' needs and interests.

When I chose to make this change and take the students seriously, they became more serious. Together we established a rubric and began a successful round of debates that concluded with an outside panel of judges scoring the debates.

I had received a gift from my students—two layers of learning about my pedagogy. The first was to include them in the problem-solving process instead of wrestling with it alone. The second was to be open to students talking about their passions and interests as an entry point into learning the curriculum. One led to the other. Both came from taking the time to talk, think, and write about why what I did worked.

A Misstep

The problem-solving model has not always worked. I tried it with another class, on a day that we were trying to learn *Romeo and Juliet* and the students were acting up. As I attempted to begin the problem-solving process, they blamed other classmates and me for their own behavior. They were rude to each other and to me, often interrupting or talking to each other while a classmate was speaking. When I admitted to being partially responsible for the problem, many launched into a scapegoat session. They told me everything they didn't like about my teaching, the classroom, and me.

I justified my actions and defended my teaching style. The more I fell into this trap, the more frustrated I became. I looked around the class and noticed that several students were disengaged from the discussion. Instead, they were engaged in the very behaviors we were trying to address! With despair, I stopped the activity.

That evening, I headed outside, my breath visible in the cold evening air, the silhouette of the tree branches highlighted against the waning moon. I tried once again to engage in the "teasing out" process about why a strategy that worked with one class was a failure with another. As I walked, I asked myself some questions. What worked? What didn't work? Where are the holes in my thinking? What did I see? What didn't I see? What can I try that I haven't tried yet? Is there something going on that I haven't paid enough attention to?

As I reviewed these questions, I realized I had skipped certain steps in the problem-solving model to save time. I hadn't required students to free write—a time for reflection that allows even the most reluctant students to share their opinions. I hadn't insisted on hearing from everyone. Further, I hadn't been specific enough in stating the problem and framing the activity for students. I had made a leap of understanding about the exercise—based on my previous successful experience—and these students, not having been there, did not leap with me.

My problem-solving repertoire was rapidly expanding. The model I had developed, created as a direct response to a classroom situation, seemed to have essential elements that needed to be included to make it work:

- Taking enough time to complete the process
- Giving students some time to digest the information and silently reflect
- Insisting on the inclusion of all voices
- Of utmost importance, allowing students to speak only about their own role in both the problem and the solution

The next day with this class, I restarted the process. I was more specific in outlining the guidelines and in describing behavior that I considered acceptable. This time the process was more successful because I had taken the time to identify what went wrong.

KEYS TO SUCCESS

As I continued to use the problem-solving model in my classes, my students became more comfortable with the concept and were more readily able to see and own to their behaviors. Over time, students even volunteered to facilitate problem-solving sessions.

What encourages my students to buy into this process? I am

explicit that we are building social skills. Students are forthcoming because they know that all students will have a chance to voice an opinion and that no one will be disregarded. They know that their teacher is engaged in this process on an equal footing. I am not imposing a solution. This model is visual and concrete, and it has a distinct beginning, middle, and end.

CHAPTER 2

The Presentation: Examining Students *At* Work

JAN GRANT

At conferences with the National School Reform Faculty and the Annenberg Institute for School Reform, session facilitators ask us to identify the one aspect of our work that we consider essential for successful teaching and learning. They also ask us to decide upon a personal priority that we believe to be a critical element for our students and for our pursuit of excellence in the teaching profession. Without wavering, I respond that the essential theme of my teaching is the creation of a safe, nonjudgmental learning environment. It is imperative that my students feel comfortable taking risks in their learning.

A colleague in the Narragansett, Rhode Island school system asked me to work with her fourth-grade class. She wanted her students to acquire the skills of process learning—skills that would enhance and improve the learning experience. Her offer provided me an opportunity to continue work on a strategy that was becoming increasingly important to me—examining students *at* work. After weeks of working with the students, they were ready to show the school and the community what they learned.

The fourth graders opened the double doors and burst into the big room holding colorful posters that described traditional lessons. With determination, they spread out to mingle with the audience of parents, teachers, and community members. They made purposeful eye contact. The sound of voices reverberated as students simultaneously articulated the words printed on their posters to as many different people as possible, saying:

We learned spelling and grammar rules
We practiced reading for comprehension and expression

Report Cards
Teamwork
Books, book reports, and dramatizations
Projects
Poetry
Math equations and problems
Theater
Field trips
There's more to writing than grammar
Homework, homework, homework
Sculpture
Each note can have a different value
Morning meetings
Library research
Et cetera, et cetera, et cetera!!

The adults and older students in the audience smiled and nodded at the high energy and enthusiasm of the fourth graders. They were familiar with the opening statements about traditional lessons of reading, writing, and arithmetic. For this evening's presentation of *Students At Work*, the cafeteria walls were papered from floor to ceiling with writing examples. Projects and subject portfolios were arranged on nine tables against the walls. Student art was everywhere. When the first chime sounded, the kids made their way to a circle of chairs in the center of the room.

In 1995, David Allen and Joe McDonald of the Coalition of Essential Schools and the Annenberg Institute of School Reform introduced a practice called "Looking At Student Work" to teachers across the country (see Allen, 1998; Blythe, Allen, & Powell, 1999). It is a practice that attempts to provide educators with new knowledge about student and teacher learning. "The Tuning Protocol" and a variety of other thoughtfully structured procedures were developed for the very close scrutiny of student work with the expectation that breakthroughs could be made about teaching and learning (see Chapter 10, Figure 10.1).

The practice of examining the work of students continues. Presently, teachers meet at conferences, at workshops, and in Critical Friends Groups to practice the protocols of "Examining Student Work" and to learn from their experience (see Chapter 7).

It is important, however, to create a connection between the product called student work and the process of students *at* work—to witness human interaction, to observe learning styles at work, to watch students during their thought processes and, on occasion, to be present for that "Aha!" moment that is so exciting.

My position in our suburban school system is as a facilitator of professional development programs and a teacher of developmental skills for the classroom. Early in the fall, Eileen Mason asked if I would visit her fourth-grade class. Eileen runs a structured, traditional classroom where the kids have the opportunity to be creative.

We met to create goals for our work together. I observed her class on three occasions to learn about the personalities and working styles of her students. Together we developed a program for her fourth-grade class that resulted in a demonstration of *Students At Work* that was presented to the community. We decided to incorporate her Social Studies teaching of Native American and Pilgrim cultures with the new process skills that I would introduce.

We identified specific outcomes to explore: the creation of a nonjudgmental atmosphere, clarity of communication, risk-taking, problem solving, facilitation, public speaking, exercising deep commitment, and understanding the pursuit of excellence. These skills spring from the foundations of the Grant Theatre Arts Process Program and such national programs as Destination Imagination and Odyssey of the Mind—all of which attract a small subset of students who are naturally attracted to that form of participation.

What was particularly exciting about this project was the opportunity to work in a heterogeneous, inclusive setting where sufficient time was designated to allow developmental skills to be mastered by the entire class. Twice a week for the next 3 months, I taught process and presentation skills to complement Eileen's teaching.

On my first day in her class, I sat with the students and Eileen in their morning circle to begin the process of creating our safe environment for open and free discussion. These students were accustomed to the "usual rules" of cooperative behavior and called these out as they had been taught at home and from the time they were in the first grade.

We should cooperate.
Classmates should be polite to one another.

Sharing is good.
Fighting is not allowed.
Meanness is not allowed.
Treat others as we want to be treated ourselves.

We initiated a discussion about school experiences where students were affected by the actions of others. At first only a few kids were willing to volunteer ideas beyond their rote learning, but as they became warmed up to the subject they were willing to describe incidents where they themselves had been hurt or where they had observed their peers shut down in class discussions as a result of negative reactions by peers or teachers. As they took part in this conversation, they laid the groundwork for creating "Group Norms," a list of expectations for behavior in the classroom (see Figure 2.1).

Later that day, the class sat with Eileen and me on the rug in the reading area and filled two chalkboards with expectations for group norms in their classroom. "No put-downs" was first on the list.

The same week, we initiated an introductory activity to practice our new norms called "Honest Talk." The first time around, the topic of "Honest Talk" should be a low-risk activity, as described in Figure 2.2.

It is designed to give students an opportunity to speak voluntarily to an audience about something in their lives. Similar low-risk activities set the stage for the conversations to follow. With the "protection" of established group norms, many students gain the courage to speak.

Figure 2.1
Group Norms

Group Norms can be defined as the rules and expectations for behavior and format that participating members decide upon prior to beginning work together. In this type of work it is important to prioritize the Group Norm so that no negative words, actions, or expressions will be tolerated. Among other "norms" this rule is established in order to create and maintain a safe environment for all participants.

Figure 2.2
Honest Talk

1. Organize the participants in a semicircle, creating a small "audience" atmosphere.
2. Choose a topic for discussion.
3. Ask for volunteers. Follow established "group norms."

In the event that a norm is broken, the facilitator calls a "time out" and the group discusses the infraction. For this class, we simply asked the students to share something they each considered special about their homes or their home environments. As time went on, topics used for discussion and the activities used to promote our goals and outcomes became more challenging.

During my time with Eileen Mason and her class, students learned to take personal and interpersonal risks. They practiced peer coaching, facilitation, improvisation, presentation skills, and new and different methods with names like "I-messaging," "Coming from Truth," "The Fishbowl," "Focus Question," "Focused Discourse," "Reflection," "Debriefing," and "Creating a Nonjudgmental Environment." Student reaction to the process was as diverse as their personalities.

Max gave me a crooked grin as I strolled over to his desk and knelt down to talk with him. His wavy hair fell onto his forehead. Max's gaze unwaveringly locked into mine. "What are you here for?" he asked. I explained that I would be teaching some lessons to go with their unit in social studies—public speaking and meeting new challenges in the classroom, for example. "When do we start? Will you be here every day? For how long? Can we miss math? Do we get to act? What are we going to do? Why are we doing this?" The questions tumbled out of Max's mouth in a rush. He had been identified as having an Attention Deficit Disorder.

Luke's wide and genuine smile was inviting. He listened well and was extraordinarily attentive while sitting with perfect posture. He raised his hand and said, "Hello, I'm Luke. I think the lessons you describe sound very interesting. I've wanted to have more challenges in school. Will there be many new projects for us to work on?" His classmates looked at Luke with approval.

Jodie sat quietly in a desk near the reading area. A cascade of long, black curls dominated her delicate face and frame. Her eyes were startling—an intense green. With hands folded, she calmly assessed the lesson. When she spoke, her voice was soft but assured and direct. "I've always wanted to do something like this—something different. When will we be able to start?"

Sam's soccer-playing talents were well known in the school. His small frame was alive with controlled energy as he sat listening intently to the lesson. With athletic gusto Sam asked, "Will this be different? Is this a social studies project that we have not done before?" He looked around the room to find a supportive look from any classmate. "Will we be working in groups? Can we play?"

Helen did not make direct eye contact, but held her head down at a slight angle and peeked at her teachers as though from around a corner. Her smile came easily, however, and she seemed quietly intrigued by what was going on. Later, during a lesson meant to motivate the level of interaction, Helen withdrew. The pace had been fast and the energy of the class was high. Helen became confused and opted to retire to a quieter place. She remained silent and did not volunteer.

The resource teacher Kerry Curren worked with several of Eileen's students in the resource room next door. Kerry asked to learn the teaching methods being used for this project in Eileen's classroom. She began to include them in her own lesson plans. This interaction provided invaluable continuity for the students. The enthusiasm of the two teachers for the project helped the kids to become motivated about this "new thing" and was indispensable to the achievement of our goals and objectives. We worked on a variety of complementary social studies lessons, process protocols, and study skills for 3 months.

As we approached the end of our allotted class time together, Eileen, Kerry, and I witnessed changes in the students. They were using facilitation and process skills that were genuinely effective and often impressive. During one of Eileen's lessons where an open discussion was underway, Sam took over as facilitator without being aware that there had been a shift in roles. Eileen began the lesson, then stepped back to watch it continue. The kids offered more in-depth opinions in class and made responsible suggestions to Eileen, Kerry, and me. With the students, we had established a safe and caring environment within the classroom. We observed a high degree of honesty in student discussions based on trust and respect. Put-downs and negative judgments were absent from the classroom. Students were learning the importance of "I-messages"—a concept described in Figure 2.3. Parents reported incidents of similar behavior at home:

> I was driving the car pool home last week when one of the usual arguments started between my son and the other two kids in the backseat. As I was about to jump in to referee, Max grinned and said to his friends, "We're being very mean to each other right now. I'll bet if we use 'I-messages' here, we wouldn't get so mad." He proceeded to teach the others what an "I-message" was and I was rendered speechless.

Eileen and I were in agreement that the hard work of the students might be highlighted by an event to culminate our time together. We thought they needed a formal closure to the project and an acknowledgment for their effort. During a brainstorm session, we decided to demonstrate our work to the public—family, friends, and the community at large.

The kids were ecstatic when they heard the idea. We formed heterogeneous groups. Eileen assigned a particular unit topic to each student. She suggested, for example, the acceptance of differences

---

Figure 2.3
"I-message"

An "I-message" is a statement that uses the personal pronoun "I" and omits the pronoun "you." A person who uses an "I-message" is taking responsibility for his or her own reactions and feelings. "You statements" can infer blame or judgment, especially in a confrontational setting.

(Adapted from *T.E.T.: Teacher Effectiveness Training* by Dr. Thomas Gordon with Noel Burch, New York: David McKay Co., 1987).

between cultures or a comparison of the status of family members in both cultures. To demonstrate the traditional unit information to their prospective "audience," each student group chose a different method. "Focused Discourse," "Improvisation," and the "Fishbowl" are examples of protocols offered for their use. We decided that the specific topic questions for the evening's lessons would not be announced to the students until the evening of the demonstration. For the community and for the students, our presentation would then be an authentic learning experience.

The decision to sponsor a presentation in the cafeteria afforded us an opportunity to help students improve their skills of projection and articulation. They practiced performance skills and learned techniques for relaxation. We observed that the possibility of public demonstration motivated and increased the level of student work ethic, and they continued to work as a true learning community. We hoped our audience would see the importance of observing students who were *at* work—learning traditional content through an unconventional process.

We had come to the night of the presentation in the cafeteria that had been transformed for the event. When the first chime rang, the students went to their seats in a center circle surrounded by the huge semicircle of their families, friends, and community members. Luke's warm smile enhanced his position as student facilitator. He stood confidently to announce the first presentation. Six students brought their chairs to form a smaller circle inside the ring of their classmates. Two extra chairs were added to the inside circle. In his starched blue shirt and colorful bow tie, Luke announced that they would be demonstrating a protocol called a "Fishbowl," as outlined in Figure 2.4.

He explained the rules to his peers as the audience listened in:

You will be given a topic to discuss that you have not rehearsed. The information for the discussion will come from what you have learned in class with Mrs. Mason. The students in the inside Fishbowl circle will have an open discussion on the topic. The people in the inner circle will take turns to volunteer information about the subject chosen for tonight's discussion. If students from the rest of the class in the outside circle choose to provide additional information on the subject, they will come to one of the empty chairs in the inside circle. After speaking,

---

Figure 2.4
Fishbowl Protocol

1. Convene a primary discussion group in a center circle with one or two empty chairs.
2. Surround the center circle with an outer group of listeners.
3. When a listener chooses to offer an idea to the discussion, he or she comes to one of the empty chairs and waits for an appropriate time to speak, and then returns to the outer circle.
4. The discussion is kept intact according to established group norms.

---

they should vacate the chairs to make room for more new kids—for more additional information. The audience will listen.

I handed Luke the slip of paper that explained the first topic of the evening: "Discuss the advantages and disadvantages that occur when diverse cultures live and work in the same neighborhood."

After a successful opening protocol, the kids beamed. They were very proud of themselves. They turned to each other and grinned. Max grinned and winked. Diminutive Jodie let out a sigh of relief. Sam jiggled happily in his chair. They were ready for anything. We sensed their anticipation for the next presentation.

An improvisation challenge was next on the agenda. Two student groups had been predetermined for this activity. See Figure 2.5 for a description of what this entailed for the students.

Outside readings and class discussions prepared the students to represent either the Native Americans or the Pilgrims in a comparative setting of a cultural activity. A printed card provided direction for the assignment they were to act out as members of different cultures. On a signal they began simultaneous performances of an improvisation to demonstrate the differences and similarities of the cultures in religious lives.

Figure 2.5
Improvisation

Improvisation is the creation or invention of a skit or recitation without preparation. An improvisational activity is one where the "actors" are given a subject or topic upon which their dialogue and/or actions are based.

Whenever possible, they were to include the relationships between the males and females in the two cultures. The girls in one group immediately sat on the floor in a circle and appeared to be engaged in food preparation. In character, they spoke quietly among themselves. The boys in that group were busily gathering some "equipment" and energetically marched off to a place where a hunt began. In the other group, it became obvious that the kids had separated themselves into groups of males, females, and children. Some of the "children" played and others seemed to be picking fruit from tall trees; the "women" sat in chairs quilting while the "men" were in a meeting of some kind. The ritual of the groups changed when one of the students chose to lead them in a new direction.

Public speaking skills were combined with the principles of "Coming from Truth" for the next format, as defined in Figure 2.6. The kids

Figure 2.6
Coming from Truth

Within a safe and nonjudgmental environment, students are encouraged to think carefully in order to define their personal opinions on a variety of subjects. Often we speak what it is we think others want to hear instead of having the courage to say what we believe.

were ready to present an "opinion" about the acceptance of *all* cultures. During class, a number of lively discussions on the subject that utilized their new communication skills had led to the consensus that being different does not mean strange or weird—it means *different*.

Every student, including Helen, participated in these conversations. At the end of one session, Sam said, "Every single person in the world wants approval, even the people we don't like. Even people not like us."

The students moved to the front of the room to recite an original piece about accepting differences. This selection had been memorized and rehearsed to present a polished effort in choral speaking (see Figure 2.7 for a description). In unison and with practiced modulation, this team told their audience that unkindness, prejudice, and racism are not innate. They are *learned*. Through public articulation, the children expressed their heartfelt wish to learn, instead, empathy and the acceptance of differences.

I looked around the room to see the audience riveted to the kids on the risers. I walked over to Eileen and rang the chime to signal the conclusion of this portion of the program.

For the rest of the evening we continued our demonstration of protocols and activities. Max facilitated what he called a "hard" vocabulary test with the audience to evaluate their concentration and comprehension. A group of students took part in a focus question protocol to explore knowledge of the differences in the environment between then and now (see Figure 2.8).

At one point, the audience was included in a question-and-answer period to determine unfounded beliefs about the period in history or the cultures being discussed.

Figure 2.7
Choral Speaking

In choral speaking, the goals are to speak in unison, to articulate vowels and consonants, and to project voices to the "back" of the room. It is an excellent method to improve enunciation in young people.

Figure 2.8
Focus Question

A question is posed. The group gathers thoughts and ideas from each other in the form of "I-messages." It is not a debate, but rather a sharing of opinion.

(Adapted from Focused Discourse Protocol as designed by Simon Hole, June 1995.)

Another demonstration took place as our activities and protocols were unfolding. A month before, Helen had confided in Kerry that she didn't think she could "do" one of these protocols in front of an audience. Kerry determined that Helen truly wanted to be involved, however. She needed to have a different kind of responsibility that was meaningful and necessary to the success of the event. Throughout the evening, we witnessed Helen, dressed in her Sunday best with clipboard in hand, happily in charge of the order, organization, and timing of events. Her position as "Coordinator" was real. Eileen, Kerry, and I observed a very special child committed to an important task and implementing it with pride.

Sam introduced the student feedback section with his usual verve. He asked his classmates:

What have you learned from this experience?
Would you use any of your new skills in other areas of your life?
What changes or additions to this type of event would make it better?

The class was now seated in a semicircle facing their audience. They responded:

It was good to be able to be in charge sometimes.
I liked it that people listened to me. I liked it that I could say things I wasn't sure of.

No one made fun of me. Ever. I wish that could happen all the
time.

I like that the superintendent and our principal came to watch
us. My father was wondering if the school committee would
be here.

Max's comment summed up the courage and honesty that he
brought to this entire project:

I think that teachers should get together from grade to grade to
plan what they teach. I've had this Pilgrim and Native American thing since the first grade.

The kids owned the evening and, besides the presentation, they
owned the skills that we ambitiously stated in our outcomes so many
months before —facilitating, adhering to group norms, creating a
nonjudgmental environment, speaking individual truths, engaging in
a demonstration of students *at* work, and practicing new methods
and protocols. We cannot leave the development of these skills to
chance. When we raise the bar, when students and teachers together
create an empathetic learning environment, and when students present
their learning to a community of respectful listeners, levels of achievements soar.

REFERENCES

Allen, D. (Ed.). (1998). *Assessing student learning: From grading to understanding.*
New York: Teachers College Press.
Blythe, T., Allen, D., & Powell, B. (1999). *Looking together at student work: A
companion guide to assessing student learning.* New York: Teachers College
Press.
Gordon, T., & Burch, N. (1987). *T.E.T.: Teacher effectiveness training.* New York:
David McKay Co.

CHAPTER 3

When Students Reflect Together: Socratic Discussions

JON APPLEBY

My work with my colleagues in Critical Friends Groups and my work with my friends in Educators Writing for Change have shaped my ability to be a reflective teacher. In both groups we work hard to say exactly what we mean, to listen to the feedback of others, and to clarify our thinking.

When our writing group gathers, the standards we apply to each other's work are "How does this incident or issue relate to the students?" and "How do these issues affect our work in the classroom?"

I began to wonder how to better engage students in this reflective process. Could my students also learn to reflect together?

At Noble High School in North Berwick, Maine, my questions led to forums we call Socratics. Students often find participation irresistible. They learn by talking to the people they find most fascinating—each other.

If Socrates were to appear in Room 126 of Noble High School and join in our discussions named for him, I feel certain he would ask me some hard questions about what might be going on there. But I would enjoy the dialogue, because what I see in Plato's renderings of the days of Socrates is one man engaged principally with one other thinker at a time, which too often is very like me in my classroom. Often *I* lead discussions, engaging one student and then the next in the hope that all present learn as they listen. Asking questions, I let students phrase their ideas, and then, like Socrates, I frequently allow myself the final word. I teach, I tell myself, by modeling. Yet one of the most difficult challenges in my classroom is to provide opportunities for reflection and speaking to the quiet students who most need the practice.

OUR SOCRATIC PRACTICES

Our junior English classes hold Socratic discussions once a week according to the rules listed in Figure 3.1. Like any other structure or protocol for conversation in the classroom, Socratics could have various possible arbitrary elements or norms. During the school year each student leads one discussion on a text of his or her choice. Each student leader is expected to come to the discussion with at least ten written questions for possible use when facilitating. Each participant is responsible for him or herself and for the progress of the group during the 30 minutes of the Socratic. Once the facilitator begins, my role as coach is to take extensive notes on what is said, noting who advances the learning and, if any, who sabotages communication with destructive behaviors.

By rule I cannot speak during the 30 minutes. Afterwards, I lead a debriefing with a specific set of questions and criteria. Later in the year, students debrief themselves. Each day one designated student charts the number of times each person speaks, with codes that indicate

---

Figure 3.1
Our Socratic Protocol

(Time limit: 30 minutes)

1. Name a facilitator, a timekeeper, and a person to chart speakers. *Specific students act as engine, rudder, or brakes.* (Remind students that time is a limited resource.)
2. Determine limits on the length of text and facilitator preparation. *Remind students that preparation in all things enhances quality.*
3. Debrief the dialogue afterwards. What was learned? Who made key contributions to the progress or lack of progress of the discussion? Give feedback to the facilitator on his or her leadership. Be specific by quoting ideas and naming individuals. *Leadership can be learned. Individuals are visible and accountable.*

whether a speaker makes a statement, asks a question, or interrupts to make a point. Early in the year I lead five or six Socratics in order to model possible texts and topics before I put students on the spot. I ask students to generate a list of positive and negative behaviors, which I then use in my observations. After each Socratic, I write a letter to the facilitator using evidence from my notes to highlight good work and work that might be improved upon. I attach my letter to my notes and to the chart of speakers and give all the paperwork to the facilitator.

Socrates had the luxury of small "classes." I don't. When I engage one student in a public dialogue, I am not necessarily engaging the other 20 to 25 students present. Although I attempt to control the pace, atmosphere, and content of my classroom—even on those rare days when I can muster the qualities and enthusiasm of great entertainers—many of my students disengage, don't concentrate, and don't explore or deepen knowledge through dialogue.

Land development and a healthy economic climate have changed Noble High School in North Berwick, Maine from what once would have been called a rural high school to a more suburban setting. But the kids I see seem to be pretty much like those anywhere else, with limited experiences of self-directed, group-driven conversations to learn together. In groups often larger than 20, extroverts struggle to control impulses while shy, worried learners, afraid they might make some kind of a mistake, often don't speak unless directly questioned, when to *not* speak would be more embarrassing than risking a comment. I ask each student to find a short text, bring it to the class, and lead a 30-minute Socratic dialogue on the ideas in the text by asking questions. The purpose of the dialogues is to search for meaning and implications in the texts. I tell my students repeatedly that all of them together should be far more knowledgeable than any one of them alone.

Part of my mission as their teacher is to help each of them know what they are like, what they actually do, in groups. I emphasize feedback and restrict my comments to perceptions after the student-led Socratic is concluded. I take copious notes and consciously hold myself as much as possible to accurately describing what I have seen, from asking questions of the participants to highlighting their behaviors, both negative and positive. I tell them that a hard question is an act of friendship.

Further, rightly or wrongly, I come to class with several other strongly held ideals about dialogue. *Listening* means that a person is willing to hear an idea and change her or his mind. *Listening* means that an individual is ready to learn. Also, in a democracy (I dream of my classroom as one) everyone needs to behave so that each voice has the chance to be heard. Healthy people control their own impulses to speak and use the feedback of others to enhance their abilities and to check their own possibly negative behaviors. When groups of people reflect together, individuals not only get valuable feedback but also have the chance to learn at an accelerated rate. Finally, in order for group work to be truly engaging and authentic, groups need to be challenged with difficult questions. I believe that learning to ask difficult questions is one of the engines that drives all learning, whether those questions are posed to others or to ourselves. I hope that I provide a forum where students can practice asking those questions.

In good moments on the best of days, students feel what it is like to extend an idea or set of ideas into what feels like new thinking. Knowledge is created or unearthed as insightful questions prod and tease the consideration of ideas. But there are also days when students' behaviors and inability to control their own intellectual environment make the achievement of new thought rare or even impossible.

I can hear Socrates now. You let kids talk for 30 minutes without intervening? You only take notes and talk about what you saw and heard afterwards? What do you do when things are said that you know to be wrong? (Socrates gets very red in the face when we talk.) You encourage the weakest thinkers and most inexperienced members of the class to choose a short text and lead the discussion? What do you do when one member of the class takes over and won't allow others to speak? What do you do when somebody takes a disputed point personally and reacts? You call this education?

My answer to this final question is yes.

A SOCRATIC

Kara had prepared two pages of quotations and ideas from *The Art of Happiness* (1998) and from the Dalai Lama for her classmates, and after giving them time to read her text, she began with her first prepared questions: "What do you think happiness is? What is happiness to you?"

Petite, with long black hair and brown eyes, an air of intense privacy and resolution about her, Kara faced her classmates, 10 males and 9 females. One of the quietest members of the class, she seemed prepared and confident. At midyear, about half the class had already taken a turn as facilitator. Seated with the students around the large table, I recorded the time and the first comments as Kara polled each participant. At first, there was silence as listeners considered her question.

Coaxed by a look from Kara, a sometimes shy and reclusive Nick began abruptly, "Because I'm not outgoing doesn't mean I'm not happy." Kara seemed dismayed at the silence that followed.

Scott (lightly glossing over Nick's interpretation of the question): Hey, I let people in in traffic.
Josh (tongue-in-cheek): Man, I got caught in downtown Sanford yesterday. People don't care.
Niomi: I let people out all the time.
Nicole grimaced: "How can you base happiness on driving? What *is* happiness?"
Jason joked: Road rage. Hah, hah.
Scott (more seriously): Material possessions play a role in happiness.
Nicole: Some people here in school have things but they aren't happy.
Scott: Well, friends are more important than possessions.

Several comments followed about the importance of cars. Kara began to look at a spot on the tabletop between Nick and her and did not look up. With her head turned slightly to the right, sitting motionlessly, her eyes seemed to trace a tight design on several inches of the table surface. In the margin of my notes I wrote in brackets: ["What happened?"]

I want to help students take control of their own learning. I think of the text, the actual discussion, the debriefing, and finally my letter to the facilitator as layers of reflection aimed at improving quality and at identifying truths. Students practice listening, speaking, and exchanging feedback about each other based upon their behaviors. People who do not speak are asked to comment in the debriefing; others who speak often and excessively are asked to consider why;

students who talk over, interrupt, or have side conversations are told how many times they do so, and who they shut out.

Echoing the students' own words, I quote excellent ideas (evidence) verbatim. Often I display strong quotations on the walls of our classroom. I applaud positive behaviors and moments of leadership. While Socratics are always about designated questions, they are also about self-recognition and change. Figure 3.2 provides a list of 10 positive Socratic behaviors that all members of the class are expected to follow—including the teacher. I like to think that the spirit of John Dewey, with his notions about the social aspects and the importance of contexts for learning, would appear to help me deal with the ghost of Socrates.

Kara's Socratic faltered as she sat looking increasingly miserable. She stared at the table and rubbed the fingertips of her left hand lightly over her list of unused questions. Many of the other participants avoided looking at her, even as several scowled in frustration at her lack of leadership. Others pressed on:

Jason: If you complain a lot, you're not happy. Some people aren't happy.
Scott: Media plays a role. You need people to talk and relate to . . . to support you.

Figure 3.2
Ten Positive Socratic Behaviors

1. Citing the text
2. Adding new information/knowledge
3. Questioning assertions
4. Supporting the points of others
5. Connecting ideas
6. Sharing examples/giving evidence
7. Sorting speakers/keeping order
8. Pointing out new or changed mindsets
9. Asking productive questions
10. Encouraging others

Ben (seated at one corner of the large table): Accomplishing a
    goal makes me happy.
Maria: All people lack certain things and when those things
    are fulfilled, they are happy.

Many students spoke at once, kidding each other about money
and their lack of it.

Maria (upset at being ignored): You're not taking this seriously.
Meagan: I think you're all focusing on being happy in the mo-
    ment. Happiness should be overall, looking back . . .
Dan: Some people can only think in the moment.
Meagan: I brought it up, that's all.

Josh described how he had changed since he met his girlfriend.
He feigned tears. Kara still stared at the table, responding neither to
serious points nor to attempts at humor.

Scott: Knowing that you love is happiness, too.
Sam: Happiness is situational. What works as a definition for
    one person doesn't necessarily work for another. Maybe
    not even for the same person at different times.
Shannon: What makes me happy changes with the mood I'm in.
Jason: Serious people aren't very happy.
Josh: Vacations put me in a good mood!
Nicole: I agree with Shannon.
Josh: I hate being alone. I can't be happy alone.
Jason: Me, either. I just get in my car and drive around.
Scott (glancing at Kara): Most people try to hide their unhappiness.
Ben: Can people learn to make themselves happy?
Josh: Happiness is pushing yourself and achieving something
    hard.
Niomi: It can also be doing something for someone else.

Similar disconnected, at times off-topic statements continued, often joking ones about dreams, money, and vehicles. Kara never spoke
before "time" was called on the Socratic. I sat looking through my
notes for almost a minute, aware of a silence. The students were
waiting to see what I would say.

I had definite opinions. Kara had bailed on her responsibility to the topic and the group, and that was not okay. Kara's body language and silence, as if disowning all comments with a kind of frozen despair, had been an impediment to the group. Josh and Jason had spent the half hour trying to come up with amusing one-liners. Although several members of the class had worked hard to keep the discussion going, principally by introducing new ideas, no one had tried to deepen ideas with follow-up questions. I thought the group avoided confronting Kara and each other. Instead of asking her for questions or asking why she withdrew, individuals pretended that everything was fine and on course when something was obviously wrong. Individuals and the group had clearly demonstrated many of the 10 negative behaviors listed in Figure 3.3. I had dozens of notes in brackets with pluses, minuses, and question marks to comment on. But I didn't.

I relied on my habitual questions, on my protocol designed to let the students bring out as many ideas as possible. I guided with questions and filled in the gaps. The benefits of a protocol, perhaps, are most keenly felt and tested when things go badly. The Socratic had been painful—in my view, a disaster. The protocol provided in Figure 3.4 would be the backbone of their attempt to figure out why.

Figure 3.3
Ten Negative Socratic Behaviors

 1. Having side conversations
 2. Making personal comments
 3. Daydreaming/being distracted
 4. Joking for attention
 5. Speaking off-topic
 6. Speaking too often
 7. Repeating opinions
 8. Using volume rather than ideas
 9. Pouting when unheard
10. Interrupting others

Figure 3.4
A List of Debriefing Questions

1. To the facilitator: How did it go? Did the text work? How many questions did you ask? Which ones energized the students?
2. To the students: Do you agree, disagree? How did it go? Be specific.
3. To the chart-keeper/note-taker: Who spoke most often today? Who was involved in side conversations? Who interrupted? Who made excellent statements, and what were they? Who didn't speak?
4. To the students who didn't speak: What did you see and hear today?

Mr. Appleby: Kara, how did it go? What went well and what didn't?

Kara: I don't know.

Mr. Appleby: How did the Socratic go? Anybody . . . ?

Niomi: We weren't in the mood . . . the topic was too deep.

Alan: I just wasn't interested. It went downhill and went slow.

Mr. Appleby: What specifically made it seem slow to you?

Alan: Well, not getting asked any questions that built on stuff just made it die . . . and die it did.

Mr. Appleby: Kara, do you think you stopped asking questions?

Kara: Yes.

Mr. Appleby: Why did you stop?

Kara: I'm having a terrible day. I just couldn't. (Kara wept, stood, and left the room. Niomi exchanged a look with me and followed Kara into the hall.)

Josh: I guess this shows how important it is to have a leader.

Mr. Appleby: Why didn't others step forward and lead when you saw Kara bail?

Shannon: That's a good point. We should have. Why didn't we?

Mr. Appleby: Once the topic is introduced and begun, is leadership shared? Is it the obligation of just one person to see to the topic?

Sam: We could see she was upset.

Mr. Appleby: Why didn't anyone address that?

Sam: You never know what answer you might get.

Maria: It's weird how we all just kept going. We were trying to be nice, to not single her out.

Mr. Appleby: Is it nice to ignore someone's discomfort?

Shannon: Isn't it easier sometimes?

Mr. Appleby: Easier for whom?

I never got a good explanation from Kara to explain her withdrawal. I settled for "personal problems" as an answer. Whether she learned or grew from that day, I have no direct evidence, but later in the school year she emerged as a speaker in Socratics and, to the amazement of everyone, read a very personal autobiographical writing out loud to the class.

That day my own ideals and protocol were tested, no doubt. During the Socratic I worried about Kara's well-being, and wanted desperately to jump in and ask Josh, for instance, if his constant joking responses were not expressions of his need to be the leader rather than real leadership. The price of giving students 30 minutes of freedom, and the responsibility of managing their own conversation and time, can often become talk about Niomi's purple Geo or the latest movie blockbuster and not the pursuit of truth.

I find myself at times desperately wanting to tell my students how they should be, rather than letting them struggle during group discussion and learn, quite often, from mistakes. I hope I am teaching them to be observant and questioning, to cite evidence for their opinions, to be both honest and tolerant, and to achieve that ideal of mine called *listening*. For me that state of *listening* is a place of potential change within us, a place where reflection and learning become both possible and powerful.

Plato doesn't really tell us about Socrates' bad days, when the noblest seeking of the good and true were muddied with the follies and limitations of human nature or the petty distractions of ancient Greek society. I seem to have those days frequently, those days when I see a few earnest swimmers trying to make headway against a tide of glib current culture. But there are also those times, often immediately after feeling tongue-tied and frustrated, when students surprisingly feel progress and see something new in the world or in themselves. I can hear that excitement in their voices and, as observer, read passionate engagement in their faces. I can see and hear them practice thinking skills—building arguments with sequenced and supported ideas, checking facts, and questioning statements of opinion—which citizens and consumers surely need. The particular nature of the text often doesn't seem important; the topic could be an ethical issue in science, an event in history, an article from the newspaper, or a poem. The key ingredient seems to be that the students know they have to rely on themselves and each other to have success.

Every year, particularly after the senior exit exhibitions that our school requires, once-quiet students thank me for using Socratics in the classroom. They know that learning to think-on-the-fly and to speak extemporaneously has prepared them to perform for that minimum 15 minutes in their senior presentations with pride and confidence. Students tell me they learned to listen, to find their voices, and to support each other—skills that help them not only in school, but in life.

REFERENCE

Dalai Lama & Cutter, H. C. (1998). *The art of happiness: A handbook for living.* New York: Putnam.

CHAPTER 4

Student-Centered Meetings: A Protocol for Working with Families

PEGGY SILVA

I smiled as I walked into my classroom on Parents' Night. Conversation stopped. All eyes faced front. Hands were folded, feet firmly placed on the floor. The cultural imprint of "school" remained strong for the adults sitting before me. I had stopped being a neighbor or a friend to the audience in front of me. I had become transformed into "the teacher," with all the associated stereotypes.

Automatic response often gets in the way of honest communication. If the purpose of meeting with parents is to improve student learning, conversations must be structured to elicit engaged responses from all parties. Toward that end, the following chapter emphasizes listening and reflection.

All transitions are messy, but the transition from childhood to adolescence can be particularly troublesome. Children know how to make eye contact, be polite to visitors, and do chores, albeit reluctantly. They respond when spoken to and communicate their plans. These behavior patterns begin to shift as children enter adolescence and begin to search for their individual identity. Although changes in behavior begin during the middle school years, these experiences can be exacerbated in the shift to a new school, to a different academic setting.

As parents cast about, searching for the cause of the massive changes they see before them, they sometimes decide that high school has stolen their children and replaced them with hostile creatures who blast loud music from behind locked doors. This rite of passage can be a difficult time for all involved. Developing the tools of dialogue and reflection can bridge communication gaps for parents who are the experts at knowing their children, teachers who are experts at the developmental stages of adolescence, and students who are the experts in reporting on their academic and social growth and struggles.

Parents' concerns shift as quickly as do the lives of their children. Suddenly, their children have learned new social codes, new dress codes, and new behavioral codes. Parents have to scramble to catch up. They have to decide whether their children can ride in a car with a 16-year-old driver. They have to decide whether their children can stay out late after a football game, whether they can go to a party at a senior's house. They have to decide whether to believe their children's claim to have no homework, or to accept their insistence that they can listen to their CD players in the classrooms. These are questions that Dr. Spock forgot to answer.

All parents and teachers were once teenagers, and we broke rules, pushed boundaries, made weird friends, took risks. We all have stories that we like to tell about our teenage years, and we have stories that we have never shared with our own parents. How scary then to know that a new generation of children is assembling an arsenal of experiences that they will keep hidden from their parents. This is the common ground of adulthood, and it is this common ground that we can use to design new communication strategies for helping our students through the rough spots in their learning.

Transition usually requires a new language, a new way of knowing. At Souhegan High School, teachers ask students to develop the habit of reflecting on their learning. We ask them to observe how they approach their work, and how satisfied they are with their own progress. We are conscious and deliberate in asking them to take note of the choices they make each day in their lives. We are trying to establish new patterns for their learning.

The dilemma we face is that we are in competition with existing communication patterns that have been in place with their parents for a lifetime. It is at this intersection that "disconnects" sometimes occur between parents and teachers, between students and parents, between teachers and students. The teachers on my ninth-grade team have begun to address this weak link through the implementation of a student-centered family meeting protocol, outlined in Figure 4.1.

Figure 4.1
Student-Centered Family Meeting Protocol

The goal of an effective family meeting is to ensure that the student, parents, and teachers exchange information regarding the student's strengths, progress, or needs. The format for this student-centered meeting ensures that the focus is on the student's performance in the classroom and as a member of our school's learning community. While there are rare occasions that a student's presence might impede the success of a meeting, we believe that it is essential for most conferences. Participants include a facilitator, teachers, counselor, student, parent/guardian, and note-taker.

(Time: 30–40 minutes)

1. The facilitator welcomes and introduces each member of the group, then outlines the protocol and the time frame, and asks one participant to serve as note-taker. (2 minutes)
2. If the meeting had been called to discuss behavioral concerns, the facilitator asks everyone to read through the appropriate behavioral guidelines. (3 minutes)
3. The facilitator speaks to the student, and asks for an update on strengths in *Course A*. What is going well in that class? Does the student understand the material? Is all work up-to-date? Is there anything that gets in the way of success in the classroom? Is the student an active participant in the class? Has the student set any goals for this course?
4. The facilitator then asks the teacher of *Course A* to join the conversation, first asking for positive reinforcement, then addressing impediments to progress. Facilitator asks for concrete suggestions from the teacher regarding how the student could improve knowledge to content, work ethic, or behavior in that particular course.

5. This process continues until the student has addressed all subjects. Parents are then asked for their thoughts about the student's performance. Questions asked and answered. (30 minutes)
6. When the student has discussed each course, and then listened to each teacher and parent, the note-taker recaps the suggested actions to be taken on the part of the student. All sign the note sheet.
7. Facilitator plans follow-up by e-mail or phone call to report progress. Facilitator reminds the student that the role of the adults present is to help the student succeed, and that the purpose of this meeting was to help the student communicate his or her progress and/or needs to teachers and to parents. (5 minutes)

A couple of years ago, our team received a frantic phone call from a mom who was very distressed at her daughter's progress report. She felt that Amy had fallen through the cracks, and that we were not paying attention to her needs. Her daughter's behavior had changed significantly at home, and although they had grounded her and instituted all sorts of social sanctions, Amy's grades continued to slip. She continued to insist that her teachers did not like her.

Until recently, their daughter had always been trustworthy and reliable, and they wanted to believe her. They had begun to wonder how her teachers had contributed to the negative changes they saw at home. Now, Amy had told her parents that one teacher had lost an important project, that another could never be found for after-school help, that another never assigned homework. Amy's mom needed help in sorting through very different information from her daughter and her daughter's teachers.

A glance at my calendar reminded me that our team had already had 11 contacts with Amy's parents. Amy's behavior and lack of progress had been the source of many phone conversations and several meetings. We had experienced a difficult time in prior meetings because her dad had dominated the conversation, preventing an easy exchange of information. We all felt on the defensive in his presence.

We knew that we needed to change the dynamic of the next meeting. This time we all needed to listen to Amy's reasons for her poor performance.

We established strong guidelines and asked all participants to agree to them at the start of the meeting. We all agreed to remain silent until the facilitator invited us into the conversation. Each of us would have the opportunity to speak and to listen.

As facilitator, I asked Amy to talk about her work in social studies. I asked her to comment on what strengths she brought to this work, what she liked about the course. I asked about her work ethic in class and in her homework. I then asked her to talk about what got in the way of her success in that class. When she had finished talking, I asked Amy's social studies teacher to comment on what he had heard in Amy's conversation. I asked him first to discuss Amy's strengths, then to comment on her performance.

We repeated that format until Amy had discussed her work in her other team courses, English, science, and math. Throughout, Amy was open and honest in assessing both her skills and her challenges. She talked about her academic strengths, and her willingness to assist others; she also discussed her lack of motivation in studying for tests or meeting deadlines, and her failure to turn in key assignments.

We then invited Amy's parents into the conversation. Her parents calmly stated that this information, coming from Amy, was a different picture than Amy had painted for them at home. They asked Amy questions to clarify what they had heard. We were silent during this exchange, "overhearing" Amy's conversation with her parents.

I joined the conversation again, asking Amy to repeat what she had heard from her teachers. She said that she had heard that they all liked her and were frustrated that she would not allow them to help her. Together, we made a list of concrete strategies to improve her performance, and established some deadlines. Another member of the team read the notes he had taken of the meeting, and we asked Amy and her parents to sign the notes. We promised that we would phone Amy's parents to discuss her progress by a certain date.

When we debriefed the process we had just engaged in, we all recognized the power of listening to Amy. She had accurately assessed her work and her behaviors. She was free of artifice in each of her conversations.

After Amy and her parents left, our team discussed what we had learned. We had observed a family dynamic at work. We had heard each other discuss the important elements of our individual classrooms. We had each heard Amy's respect for us. We had seen Amy's parents listen to her. We had created a safety zone for effective communication.

Following the meeting with Amy and her parents, our team began to operate all of our parent meetings with a strong student-centered focus. We are fortunate to have common planning time to meet with our teammates, to schedule parent meetings, and to meet with our students outside of our classrooms. We developed a formal protocol for all parent meetings, adding the component of using our school's code of behavior to address behavioral concerns.

Our team meets with parents for a variety of reasons. Sometimes, parents want to meet us to get a sense as to whether their child is being well served in our classes. Sometimes parents want to meet to clear up a misunderstanding over an assignment. Most of our meetings, however, stem from a lack of open communication between the parent and the child. When teachers meet with students and parents separately, this communication gap widens. Like the childhood game of telephone, stories change when repeated from person to person. The most effective communication strategy, therefore, is to have all essential parties present at the same time and for all to have an equal opportunity to speak and to listen.

This does not happen in most settings. Typically, responding to a request by a concerned parent, counselors or administrators summon teachers to attend a hastily assembled meeting. Their participation is based solely on the intersection of their names on a particular student's schedule. Their purpose is to offer input regarding the student's progress and/or behavior in an individual course. If students are present at all, they are usually silent or sullen. The format of this type of meeting frequently elicits a defensive posturing by the teacher(s), the parents, or both. There is no explicit agreement about the expected outcome of the meeting except to fix a problem. Implicit in this setup is that somebody has caused the problem. No one expects a long-term solution, just a quick fix to that day's dilemma.

It can be very intimidating for parents to walk into a classroom, to approach a table of teachers, to listen as each searches through the particular hieroglyphics of individual grade books to provide information on a child's performance. It can be difficult to discern what the rules are for the conversation. Parents' frustrations stem from a sense of unequal membership at the table.

If our mutual goal is to improve student learning, we cannot omit students from the equation. Students cannot be silent observers as we discuss their progress. By placing the student at the center of the conversation, we level the playing field. By providing a structured format for dialogue and facilitation, we remain focused on the goal of improving student learning. Parents and teachers all listen to what matters to our students, and we all hear this information at the same moment.

It is difficult and awkward to implement new communication strategies. It is much easier for a teacher to flip open a ledger and spew out lists of missing assignments and grades. It is much easier for a parent to charge a teacher with a lack of attention or to accuse a teacher of unfair practices. Changing a prevailing culture of finger-pointing and blame-placing can be an agonizing endeavor. However, if parents and teachers can collaborate on building and reinforcing skills of advocacy and reflection in their students, they foster a spirit of collegiality. A student-centered approach to family meetings is a worthy first step.

CHAPTER 5

Storytelling and the Art of Reflective Conversation

S̲ɪᴍᴏɴ H̲ᴏʟᴇ

I think of myself as a teacher and as a storyteller. My fourth-grade classroom in Narragansett, Rhode Island, provides ample stories. My teaching partner and I have spent the last 10 years examining our practice—observing our students and the work they produce. We spend much time reflecting on what happens in our classrooms.

I began writing these stories of our reflecting to share with my colleagues in EWC. Both my teaching practice and my stories have benefited. Receiving feedback on the words I've put on paper has sharpened my writing. More important, it has sharpened both my stories and my ability to reflect on my practice.

My colleagues have impressed upon me the importance of taking my stories to a wider audience. The following chapter tells the story of what happened when I began a new level of sharing, much like the people Freire (1994) describes: "At the point of encounter there are neither utter ignoramuses nor perfect sages; there are only people who are attempting, together, to learn more than they now know" (p. 71).

In many schools, the only points at which teachers encounter each other are lunchrooms and hallways, and in either case the conversation rarely goes beyond "Have you seen that new movie?" or "How about those Red Sox?" Too often, even staff development days are spent listening to someone who wishes to tell teachers how things should be done. As we struggle to create professional learning communities in schools, we would be wise to create points of encounter, places where teachers might engage in a reflective dialogue that would allow all to learn more than they now know.

A POINT OF ENCOUNTER

On Tuesday morning we straggle in an hour before the students arrive, coffee cups filled, the caffeine yet to kick in. The six of us sit at hexagonal tables in chairs built for 9-year-olds, talking quietly. We hear rushed footsteps in the hallway, and Annie begins speaking before she seats herself. "Thanks for the story, Simon. Just what I needed this time of year. More tension!"

Annie and the others had gathered as part of an ongoing professional development project—the focus group. Originally conceived during a course in qualitative research methodology, the group consisted of five to seven teachers and administrators who met on a monthly basis. Although membership in the group changed over the course of the year, the purpose remained the same—to explore the nature of teaching and learning. We met not to tell others what should be, but to think together about what is and to imagine what could be. The goal was professional growth for all participants. (See Figure 5.1 for tips on how to convene your own focus group.)

Prior to each meeting I passed out a short vignette we would use to focus our conversations. These stories of life in the classroom focused on the decisions teachers make, and they often dealt with the moral and ethical dilemmas that are a part of daily life in classrooms.

Figure 5.1
Convening a Focus Group

- Invite five or six colleagues. Too many participants means less time for everyone to speak.
- Find people willing to listen hard and respond with their thoughts and stories.
- Let them know exactly what to expect and what the purpose is and isn't.
- Try to get a variety of people—look outside your department, grade level, and circle of friends.

This time, Annie was responding to my story, "Taking Care of Terry," a fictionalized account of several classroom events. It proved to be a most powerful tale.

TAKING CARE OF TERRY

The thing is, Terry is very fragile. His home life is in shambles, and his self-concept is as low as I've seen in my 20 years of teaching. Oh, he keeps up a brave front, a gruff front. He likes to be at the center of attention, and is in fact looked up to by many of his classmates. But it's an act. Having spent a year with him, I really know Terry, and how much he hurts. He's a bright kid in many ways, most of which won't help him get through school. He has the ability to connect ideas in remarkable ways—ways quite different from the typical twelve-year-old. But he has difficulty translating his thoughts into writing, and his reading skills are well below level. Actually, his comprehension is fine, but the reading itself is slow and awkward, and he often gives up. He knows this about himself. He has said to me, "I'm stupid. I can barely get through some of these books we read." So I've really tried this year to find ways for Terry to meet with success. And sometimes to protect him from failure.

Knowing how Terry hates to read out-loud to the group, I was shocked to see his hand go up when I asked for volunteers. We were planning our class's part in the end-of-year celebration. As the oldest students in the school, each sixth-grade class had been asked to write an essay entitled "We Remember." We finished writing our essay and decided to randomly select a person to read it at the assembly. The names of the volunteers were to be placed in a hat. I started walking among the desks, collecting the slips of paper and depositing them in Mike's baseball hat.

By the time I got to Terry's desk, my mind was racing: "He's being macho here. He knows this is a prestige thing, and he likes to be at the center. Does he really know what he's volunteering for? Does he honestly think he could get up in front of the school and read this? Maybe if we had more time, but

the ceremony is tomorrow! Why didn't I get started on this earlier? If only I had time to coach him! What if his name gets
pulled out? What if he freezes in front of the school? Is he
ready for this? Will it cause him more harm than good?"

Terry was last. Without quite knowing what I would do, I
took his slip of paper and, walking to the front of the room,
put my hand into the hat. As I stood there, shaking the hat
above my head with one hand and calling on Marie to come
select the lucky reader, my other hand slipped into my pocket
and deposited Terry's chance. When Anna's name was read,
the other volunteers moaned good-naturedly. They knew that
pulling out of the hat was fair. I thought I saw a look of relief
on Terry's face as I walked to my desk and deposited six slips
of paper into the trash. Terry's slip would stay in my pocket
till the students had left for lunch. Then, in an empty room, it
would take its place with the others.

EXPERIENCE AS STORY

When I first wrote "Taking Care of Terry" and before I used it with
the focus group, I shared it with a group of colleagues at a retreat.
After passing it out, I stepped onto the porch while they read and
gathered their thoughts. Soon the door flew open and JoAnne rushed
out, her voice rising as she approached me. "Is this you? Did you do
this? How could you!"

JoAnne's moral outrage is a common reaction to "Taking Care of
Terry." It is not the kind of experience we like to share. Yet we've all
been there in one way or another, all done or said something that,
upon reflection, we wish we could take back, something that flies in
the face of everything we believe about teaching. Our first reaction
to these experiences is to bury them deeply within ourselves where
they trouble our dreams.

Dewey (1938) reminds us that, "Every experience is a moving
force. Its value can be judged only on what it moves toward and into"
(p. 38). To set any of our experiences aside is to lessen their value.
How might they become "moving forces" for our professional growth?

The focus group provided a place to tell the stories of our daily
lives and to mine them for whatever learning we could find. We

learned the art of storytelling so that these narratives might open the door to reflection. However, the sharing of experiences must be paired with listening—a thoughtful, reflective examination of the stories being told. (If convening your own focus group, you may find it useful to follow a set of group norms such as the ones listed in Figure 5.2.)

A SEARCH FOR MEANING

For this meeting of the focus group, Annie's lament began our search. "Thanks for the story, Simon. Just what I needed this time of year. More tension!"

The laughter that follows feels strained, and while we will loosen up as the conversation progresses, there is an edge to it, as if Terry's story has cut just a bit too closely to the nightmare that teaching can become. Several in the group have an angry tone, initially directed toward the teacher who had "stolen Terry's chance, maybe his life." But the anger is also directed toward the system—the norms and structures that seem to force us into decisions such as these.

Many of the initial comments are attempts to provide Terry's teacher with alternatives. "He could have helped Terry. He could have spent the rest of the day going over the reading. He could have called home and gotten the parents to help. Other students could have played the role of audience." The tone of voice that carries these statements

---

Figure 5.2
Set of Group Norms

- Listen hard and actively—ask questions if you don't understand.
- Respect others' opinions and ideas.
- Give voice to your own thoughts and stories.
- What is said here, stays here.
- Watch your "airtime."

seems to say this is what should have been, rather than what could have been.

Ellen breaks through the "it should have been" phase. She leans back in her chair, talking more to herself than to the group, telling a story of one of her students. "Billy is like Terry, only I have to spend 50 percent of my time with him. I know it's not fair to the other students, and I know I should be sending him to the Special Ed Behavior room, because that's what his Individual Education Plan calls for. But every time I do that, I feel like a failure."

As in all the focus groups, the participants eventually tell tales of their own teaching. In the first meeting, one teacher told how her first graders were unable to vote on merit instead of popularity, which led another to tell of how she had sometimes "fixed" elections, which opened the floodgates of my own memories, and led directly to the writing of "Taking Care of Terry." Stories lead to stories lead to stories, each carrying us closer to some clearer sense of who we are as teachers. (When your group is ready to prepare stories for sharing, consider the guidelines listed in Figure 5.3.)

Mike's response to Ellen's story is anger. He leans forward, his voice rising, gesturing to the group. "You are not a failure. It's the system that's failing. There is something wrong with a system that views mistakes as failures. If this kid gets up on the stage and doesn't read very well, maybe even can't finish the piece, the system says he

---

Figure 5.3
Telling Stories

- Some people prefer to write their stories out—others will want to tell them orally.
- Practice telling your story several times before preparing your final version.
- Keep it short. Anything over two or three pages or 5 minutes is probably too long.
- Don't worry too much about details. If you leave out anything important, the participants will ask.

failed. How can we learn from our mistakes if mistakes are seen as evidence of failure?" Mike is talking of Terry, but he is also talking of us all—as teachers, are we allowed to fail? Do we allow ourselves to fail?

The picture of Terry's failing on stage leads Louise to wonder just who is on stage, anyway. "When our Terrys get up on that stage and perform well, we feel proud. But if they fail, well, we fail, too."

Rita ponders the implications of Louise's statement, asking, "Is there a part of me that's up on the stage with Terry? Is it possible to ever remove a part of us from that success, that failure?"

The conversation swings back and forth, several themes weaving themselves into a tapestry of reflection. The responses to the ethical question raised by Terry's story fall into two camps. There are those who feel unequivocally that the teacher was wrong, that no matter what, he should have placed Terry's name into the hat. "I could sympathize with the teacher, I really could. It's obvious that he cares about Terry, that he wants to protect him. But in the end, he's passing judgment and sentencing Terry." Some aren't so forgiving of the teacher. "I'm not sure that you can protect somebody from failing. If you do that, then maybe you're not really teaching."

Others can't see it as a black and white issue and struggle to explain their mixed feelings. "I think it was a mistake for him not to put Terry's name in the hat, but I might have done the same thing. In fact, I have done the same thing. When the girl who wants to try out for the lead part in the play has a voice that is too soft, I push her to be one of the chorus. Is that so different from keeping her name out of the hat? Don't we all do this stuff? Don't we all sometimes do whatever we have to do to ensure that our kids don't fail?"

Individual stories continue to find their way to the table as the teachers make new connections. Connie worries about how, in an attempt to protect kids from failure, we may end up doing more harm than good. "I'm sure my son's teachers were trying to be kind, to build him up. But when they told him his work was 'good,' he knew it wasn't. He may have had a learning disability, but he wasn't stupid. He's twenty-seven now, and still talks about how his first-grade teachers lied to him. I try very hard not to do that to my students."

Diane sums up many of these feelings while at the same time telling how she is affected by the need to take care of her students. "I see myself as having to be the teacher, the counselor, the therapist, the mother. The children's needs are just unbelievably intense. So sometimes I find myself doing things and thinking, 'Am I doing a little God thing here?' You know, the boy comes in and says his father hit him and I want to fix it. I want to take away those hurts. I want to make that better. So it's like a savior thing."

Annie, who began the conversation, has the last word, saying, "This is the kind of thing that stays with us. We may not think much of it right away, given the constant demands on our time during the school day. But once we get home, once we sit down and let ourselves remember the day, it is there. And it stays there until the next thing comes along and crowds it out."

(It is useful for groups doing this kind of work to follow a process for group reflection such as the one highlighted in Figure 5.4.)

LEARNING MORE

This kind of collegial reflection is unusual in schools, widely acknowledged as consisting mostly of individuals thinking and acting alone. Not that teachers don't share the events of their daily lives; the walls of faculty lounges have witnessed the telling of many a tale. However,

---

Figure 5.4
Focus Groups: The Process

1. If possible, pass out one story the day before the meeting.
2. Plan for 45 minutes to an hour for one story. Supply food and drink.
3. Some people like to have a focusing question. Others prefer to start more generally. What do you think? Or what does this story say to you?
4. After you've told your story, become a listener. Avoid answering anything but clarifying questions.
5. Ask questions. Try to help the participants to think further.
6. Become a part of the group searching together for a clearer sense of what it means to be a teacher.

the common culture of schools requires that our responses to such tales be limited to wise nods or clucks of sympathy.

Telling our stories is hard. The uncertainty surrounding the point of encounter screams at us to hold back, to keep the tales to ourselves. Better to bury the story within than to risk the unknown. But without this risk taking, there is no growth.

Like all forms of reflective practice, storytelling begins by paying close attention to experience as it is lived. We must learn to pay special attention to those events that seem incongruous, that leave us thinking, "What was going on there?" We need to listen to the little voice within that says, "Pay attention here, something important is happening."

Once the story is found, storytelling requires a willingness to share those experiences with others. It requires an openness that encourages others to tell their stories as they arise. It requires a desire to search for the value of experiences. It is difficult work, requiring much time and a high tolerance for risk. The learning and growth that occur as multiple voices join in searching conversation is worth the effort. We must continue to attempt, together, to learn more than we now know.

REFERENCES

Dewey, J. (1938). *Experience and education.* New York: Macmillan.
Freire, P. (1994). *Pedagogy of the oppressed.* New York: Continuum.

CHAPTER 6

Reflection Is at the Heart of Practice

SIMON HOLE AND GRACE HALL MCENTEE

Our hearts tell us we must slow down, look carefully at events that comprise our lives in school, and consider the implications for our teaching. Yet our minds are so often focused on the lesson at hand, we leave ourselves no time for reflection.

Two of us—Simon and Grace—felt strongly that we needed to examine more closely and think more deeply about the details of our practice. Each month Grace coached Simon's Critical Friends Group at Narragansett Elementary School. Once a week Simon observed Grace's students at Pilgrim High School, in Warwick, Rhode Island. We shared the stories of our professional lives, both verbally and in writing. We explored the events behind the stories, constantly asking "Why?" and "What does it mean?"

Eventually, as we puzzled out the meanings of what we shared, we thought how others might benefit from knowing our reflective process. Over the course of a year the following chapter was born. It was not an easy birth. As teachers, we were both used to collaboration. As writers, we found it difficult to settle into a style that would incorporate both our voices.

From our own volumes of written and unwritten stories, we—a fourth-grade teacher and a high school teacher—chose two incidents. As usual, each of us used a protocol to formalize the process of thinking more deeply about what happened in the classroom.

This chapter is an expanded version of "Reflection Is the Heart of Practice" by Simon Hole and Grace Hall McEntee, May 1999, *Educational Leadership, 59*(6), pp 28–31. Copyrighted © 1999 by the Association for Supervision and Curriculum Development. Reprinted with permission from ASCD. All rights reserved.

A protocol, or guide, enables us to refine the process of reflection, alone or with colleagues. Simon chose a protocol developed during our work together. The Guided Individual Reflection Protocol is particularly useful for those who choose to reflect alone. Grace chose the Critical Incidents Protocol, developed through her work with the Annenberg Institute for School Reform at Brown University and used for shared reflection. The steps for each protocol are similar. Both include writing.

GUIDED REFLECTION

Simon follows the Guided Individual Reflection Protocol shown in Figure 6.1 as he examines an incident from his classroom.

Step 1. Collect Stories

For Simon the first step in guided reflection is to collect possible episodes for reflection. David Tripp (1993) encourages us to think about ordinary events, which often have much to tell us about the underlying trends, motives, and structures of our practice. The story that follows, "The Geese and the Blinds," exemplifies this use of an ordinary event.

Step 2. What Happened?

> Wednesday, September 24, 9:30 a.m. I stand to one side of the classroom, taking the morning attendance. One student glances out the window and sees a dozen Canada geese grazing on the playground. Hopping from his seat, he calls out as he heads to the window for a better view. Within moments, six students cluster around the window. Others start from their seats to join them. I call for attention, ask them to return to their desks. When none of the students respond, I walk to the window and lower the blinds.

Answering the question, "What happened?" is more difficult than it sounds. We all have a tendency to jump into an interpretive or judgmental mode, but it is important to begin by simply telling the story. Writing down what happened—without analysis or judgment—aids in creating a brief narrative. Only then are we ready to move to the third step.

Figure 6.1
Guided Individual Reflection Protocol

1. *Collect Stories.* Some find that keeping a set of index cards or a steno book close at hand provides a way to jot down stories as they occur. Others prefer to wait until the end of the day and write in a reflective journal.
2. *What Happened?* Choose a story that strikes you as particularly interesting. Write it out in as succinct a fashion as possible.
3. *Why Did It Happen?* Fill in enough of the context to give the story a sense of meaning. It is impossible to include all the background. Answer the question in a way that makes sense to you.
4. *What Might it Mean?* Recognizing that there is no one answer to this question is an important step. This should be an attempt to explore possible meanings rather than a presentation of what the meaning must be.
5. *What Are the Implications for Practice?* Again, this step is about exploring the possibilities. Tell how your practice might change given any new understandings that have emerged from the earlier steps.

(Adapted from the Critical Incidents Protocol [see Figure 6.2] by Simon Hole and Grace Hall McEntee)

Step 3. Why Did it Happen?

Attempting to understand why an event happened the way it did is the beginning of reflection. We must search the context within which the event occurred for explanations. Simon reflects:

> It's not hard to imagine why the students reacted to the geese as they did. As nine-year-olds, they are incredibly curious about their world. Explaining my reaction is more difficult. Even as I was lowering the blinds, I was kicking myself. Here

was a natural opportunity to explore the students' interests. Had I stood at the window with them for five minutes, asking questions to see what they knew about geese, or even just listening to what they might have to say, I'd be telling a story about seizing the moment, or taking advantage of a learning opportunity. I knew that even as I lowered the blinds. So, why?

Searching deeper, we may find that a specific event serves as an example of a more general category of events. We need to consider the underlying structures within the school that may be a part of the event and examine deeply held values and beliefs. As we search, we often find more questions than answers.

Two key things stand out concerning that morning. First, the schedule. On Wednesdays, students leave the room at 10:00 a.m. and do not return until 15 minutes before lunch. I would be out of the classroom all afternoon attending a meeting, and so this half hour was all the time I would have with my students.
Second, this is the most challenging class I've had in 22 years of teaching. The first 3 weeks of school had been a constant struggle as I tried strategy after strategy to hold their attention long enough to have a discussion, give directions, or conduct a lesson. The hectic schedule and the need to prepare the class for a substitute added to the difficulty I've had "controlling" the class, so I closed the blinds.

There's something satisfying about answering the question, "Why did it happen?" Reflection often stops here. If the goal is to become a reflective practitioner, however, we need to look more deeply. The search for meaning is step four of the process.

Step 4. What Might it Mean?

Assigning meaning to the ordinary episodes that make up our days can feel like overkill. Is there really meaning behind all those events? Wouldn't it be more productive to wait for something extraordinary to happen, an event marked with a sign: "Pay attention! Something important is happening." Guided reflection is a way to find the meaning within the mundane. Split-second decision making is a crucial aspect of teaching. Given the daily madness of life in a classroom, considering all the options and the consequences is difficult. Often it is only through reflection that we even recognize that we had a choice, that we could have done something differently.

> Like a football quarterback, I often make bad decisions because of pressure. Unlike a quarterback, I don't have an offensive line to blame for letting the pressure get to me. While it would be nice to believe that I could somehow make the pressure go away, the fact is that it will always be with me. Being a teacher means learning to live within that pressure, learning from the decisions I make, and learning to make better decisions.

Our growing awareness of how all events carry some meaning is not a new concept. John Dewey (1938) wrote about experience and its relationship to learning and teaching: "Every experience affects for better or worse the attitudes which help decide the quality of further experiences" (p. 37). He believed that teachers must be aware of the "possibilities inherent in ordinary experience . . ." (p. 89), that "the business of the educator [is] to see in what direction an experience is heading" (p. 38). Rediscovering this concept through the examination of ordinary events creates a fresh awareness of its meaning.

The search for meaning is an integral part of being human. But understanding by itself doesn't create changes in classroom practice. The last phase of guided reflection is more action oriented and involves holding our practice to the light of those new understandings.

Step 5. What Are the Implications for Practice?

Simon continues:

> My reaction to the pressure this year has been to resort to methods of control. Why did I pull down the blinds? The easy answer is that I was trying to control the situation, to get the kids back in their seats so they could listen to directions.
>
> On another level, pulling down the blinds may have been an attempt at self-control. With so much going on in my teaching world, I had no space for even a 10-minute digression into the students' world. In this sense, the blinds were falling between the students and me.

So, I'm thinking about how I might better deal with the pressure. But there is something else that needs attention. Where is the pressure coming from? I'm sensing from administration and parents that they feel I should be doing things differently. I've gotten subtle and overt messages that I need to pay more attention to "covering" the curriculum, that I should be finding a more equal balance between process and product.

Maybe they're right. What I've been doing hasn't exactly been a spectacular success. But I think that what is causing the lowering of the blinds stems from my not trusting enough in the process. Controlling the class in a fairly traditional sense isn't going to work in the long run. Establishing a process that allows the class to control itself will help keep the blinds up.

Cultivating deep reflection through the use of a guiding protocol is an entry into rethinking and changing practice. Alone, each of us can proceed step by step through the examination of a particular event. Through the process, we gain new insights into implications of ordinary events, as Simon did when he analyzed the incident of "The Geese and the Blinds."

CRITICAL INCIDENTS

While Guided Individual Reflection is for use by individuals, the Critical Incidents Protocol is used with colleagues. The goal is the same: to get to the heart of our practice, the place that pumps the lifeblood into our teaching, where we reflect, gain insight, and change what we do with our students. In addition, the Critical Incidents Protocol encourages the establishment of collegial relationships.

Schools are social places. Although too often educators think and act alone, in most schools colleagues do share daily events. Stories told in teachers' lounges are a potential source of rich insight into issues of teaching and learning and can open doors to professional dialogue.

Telling stories has the potential for changing individual practice and the culture of our schools. The Critical Incidents Protocol allows practitioners to share stories in a way that is useful to their own thinking and to that of the group. Figure 6.2 provides a summary of the steps involved in this protocol.

The steps in the process of reflection as a group are almost identical to those for reflecting alone. Reviewing the process that Simon describes will be helpful in preparing for the one that follows.

The purpose for this process is to learn together by using an

---

Figure 6.2
Critical Incidents Protocol for Shared Reflection

1. *Getting Started.* The group assigns roles: facilitator, time-keeper, etc.
2. *Write Stories.* Each member of the group writes briefly in response to the question: What happened? (10 minutes)
3. *Choose a Story.* The group decides which story to use.
4. *What Happened?* Presenter reads the written account of what happened and sets it within the context of professional goals or outcomes on which he or she is working. (10 minutes)
5. *Why Did it Happen?* Colleagues ask clarifying questions about what happened or about why the incident occurred. (5 minutes)
6. *What Might it Mean?* The group raises questions about what the incident might mean in the context of the presenter's work. They discuss as professional, caring colleagues. Presenter listens. (15 minutes)
7. *What Are the Implications for Practice?* Presenter responds, then the group engages in general conversation about what the implications might be for the presenter's practice and for their own. A useful question at this stage might be, "What new insights occurred?" (15 minutes)
8. *Debrief the Process.* The group talks about what just happened. How did the process work? (10 minutes)

(Derived from the work of David Tripp by Grace Hall McEntee during her work with Annenberg Institute for School Reform.)

incident as the catalyst for group reflection. For this protocol three to five colleagues agree to meet for the purpose of exploring a critical incident, which Tripp (1993) defines as an event that is "commonplace" and that is "rendered critical through analysis" (p. 13).

Step 1. Getting Started

Each participant will have a copy of the protocol. An appointed facilitator from the group will keep the process flowing. Specific times are allotted for each step of the process. Strict adherence to these times reins in individuals who are unaccustomed to thinking about their own airtime and assures those gathered of completing the task within a given period of precious time.

Step 2. Write Stories

For 10 minutes, each participant writes a brief account of an incident that has occurred within the school or classroom. Colleagues should know that the sharing of their writing will be for the purpose of getting feedback on what happened rather than on the quality of the writing itself.

Step 3. Choose a Story

The sharing of individual stories raises issues in the fresh air of collegial support. If open dialogue is not already part of a school culture, however, colleagues may feel insecure about sharing their own stories. To gain confidence, they may choose to run through the protocol first with a story that is not theirs. For this purpose Grace offers a story from her practice as a high school English teacher (See Step 4).

The group decides which story to use with the protocol for this particular session. The facilitator may ask for a quick go-round of summaries (2 minutes each, for example) to create a pool of possibilities. It is important to remember that each story is worthy, even though it emerges from an ordinary incident that shows barely a ripple in the everyday life at school.

Once the group decides which story to use for this session, the presenter reads the story aloud. The other participants listen carefully to understand what happened. If the group is ready to fly on its own, following the steps in the Critical Incidents Protocol will provide a guide to the process. If not, someone in the group will become "Grace" and the group will work with the following story.

Step 4. What Happened?

Grace's story:

> We went into the computer lab to work on essay drafts. TJ, Neptune, Ronny, and Mick sat as a foursome. Their sitting together had not worked last time. On their single printer an obscene message had appeared. All four had denied writing it.
>
> The next day Ronny, Neptune, and Mick had already sat down. Just as TJ was about to take his seat, I asked him if he would mind sitting over at the next bay of computers. He exploded. "You think I'm the cause of the problem, don't you?"
>
> Actually I did think he might be, but I wasn't at all certain. "No," I said, "but I do want you to sit over here for today." He got red in the face, plunked down in the chair near the three other boys, and refused to move.
>
> I motioned for him to come with me. Out in the hall, I said to him quietly, "The bottom line is that all of you need to get your work done."
>
> Out of control, body shaking, TJ angrily spewed out, "You always pick on me. Those guys . . . You . . . " I could hardly hear his words, so fascinated was I with his intense emotion and his whole body animation.
>
> Contrary to my ordinary response to students who yell, I felt perfectly calm. I knew I needed to wait. Out of the corner of my eye, I saw two male teachers rise out of their chairs in the hallway about 25 feet away. They obviously thought that I, a woman of small stature, needed protection. But I did not look at them; I looked at TJ and waited.
>
> When he had expended his wrathful energy, I said softly, "You know, TJ, you are a natural-born leader." I waited. Breathed in and out. "You did not choose to be a leader; it was thrust upon you. But there you are. People follow you. So you have a tremendous responsibility, to lead in a positive and productive way. Do you understand what I am saying?"
>
> Like an exhalation after a long in-breath, his body visibly relaxed. He looked down at me and nodded his head. Then, he held out his hand to me and said, "I'm sorry."
>
> Back in the room, he picked up his stuff and, without a word, moved to the next bay of computers.

Step 5. Why Did It Happen?

Colleagues ask clarifying questions about what happened or why the incident occurred. These are the same kinds of questions that Simon asked himself during his guided reflection. Now, however, the group has the opportunity to think collaboratively. Every question that emerges from the activity is a question not only about "Grace's" practice, but about that of each member of the group. If left unexamined, these events sometimes lead to an erosion of hopes and ideals upon which individuals and faculties build educational practice. Staying with the "why," asking it over and over, leads to the uncovering of layers.

At first you'll think you need more information than this, but we think you have enough here. Your "Grace" can answer clarifying questions about what happened or why it happened in whatever way he or she sees fit.

Step 6. What Might It Mean?

After the "why's" have been exhausted, group members discuss what the incident might mean in terms of "Grace's" or another presenter's practice. During this portion of the protocol, the presenter listens and takes notes. The taking of notes has a calming effect. It removes the need for the presenter to feel defensive.

Step 7. What Are the Implications for Practice?

During this phase of the process, the presenter responds to partici-pants' comments about what the incident might mean in terms of a particular individual practice. The facilitator assists in the transition from this individual response to a group dialogue around this kind of incident and the implications it might have for any practice.

Step 8. Debrief the Process

The debriefing is an essential part of the Critical Incidents Protocol, as it provides members with an opportunity to critique the process. The facilitator or another member of the group leads a conversation about what happened during the session, how well the process worked, and how the group might change the process for the next round.

Using the Critical Incidents Protocol becomes a different experi-ence when the group consists of members who are not colleagues—

parents and/or teachers and administrators from across the district or from out of state. With groups whose members live and work outside a particular school culture, the process often reveals stunning insights into school culture and professional practice.

THE HEART OF TEACHING AND LEARNING

Whether you use the "Guided Individual Reflection Protocol" for individual reflection or the "Critical Incidents Protocol" for group reflection, whether you use an incident by yourself or with a group, we believe that building reflective practice is a sure way to get to the heart of teaching and learning.

REFERENCES

Dewey, J. (1938). *Experience and education*. New York: Macmillan.
Tripp, D. (1993). *Critical incidents in teaching: Developing professional judgement*.
    New York: Routledge.

CHAPTER 7

Linking Student Learning to Teacher Practice through Critical Friends Groups

Peggy Silva

You name the buzz words—this unit was solid gold. When asked to bring a piece of curriculum to examine with several colleagues, I knew exactly which unit to bring —interdisciplinary, heterogeneous, full inclusion, authentic assessment. I knew my colleagues would affirm my effort and my intent with this piece of curriculum. I needed that affirmation for the first time I shared my work with others.

Twelve colleagues who taught art, social studies, math, science, and English provided warm feedback and posed questions aimed at helping me see my work. Nobody told me what I should change. Nobody criticized my work or me. They all focused on my needs. Their thoughtful questions helped me to see concrete ways to improve student learning in this already strong unit. I wondered if this same group could help me with work that I was not at all sure about.

The following chapter describes the process of reflective practice through the lens of one teacher at one high school in Amherst, New Hampshire.

As teachers, we ask questions of ourselves everyday as we prepare our work with our students. We wonder why something works with one group yet not another; we devise different ways of introducing content; we explore new ideas gained at workshops and in graduate courses; we revise and refine our tests and quizzes. Often, this work is done in isolation. And although our questions are constant, we seldom have sustained time to reflect and focus on our work, let alone perform serious research to improve student learning. This is not work that can happen at the end of a school day as we lug home heavy briefcases filled with student papers, or race to daycare to pick up our own youngsters, or head to the sports fields or theater to coach extracurricular activities. Reflection and analysis can only happen with a sustained focus that encourages the same academic rigor that characterizes our relationships with our students.

SUSTAINED FOCUS ON PROFESSIONAL DEVELOPMENT

Sustained focus on professional development to improve student learning happens in our school through our membership in Critical Friends Groups (CFGs). Mandatory for all members of our professional staff (and optional for members of our support and paraprofessional staff), CFGs meet during monthly delayed opening days at our high school. CFGs provide the structure, resources, and time to improve our skills and enhance student learning.

An initiative developed by the Annenberg Institute for School Reform, and now part of the National School Reform Faculty (NSRF), Critical Friends Groups consist of small groups of educators who engage in collaborative study with the goal of improving student learning and teacher practice. Within a CFG, practitioners learn and practice techniques for examining student work and observing their colleagues at their work. They discuss articles from professional journals. They learn strategies for requesting and receiving feedback on curriculum and assessment design. CFG colleagues help each other make choices as to how to introduce concepts to students and how to find evidence that the students have learned the concepts taught. CFGs also offer assistance to members who are performing research based on inquiry questions that stem from their work. (For more information on Critical Friends Groups, contact www.nsrfharmony.org.)

I often do not see members of my CFG during my school day, but at our monthly meetings they help to challenge my thinking. As professional colleagues they do not have to sift through additional filters of close friendship—they simply have to believe that I am serious in my intent to improve my work. Since my CFG colleagues represent artistic, mathematical, scientific, athletic, and technological intelligences, they offer me the gift of seeing my work through these lenses. In addition, some provide insight into helping students who have complex learning or emotional difficulties.

Examples of CFGs at Work

Our CFGs are as heterogeneous as our classrooms, so I must acknowledge my vulnerability as I attempt to help others through their dilemmas. When Jim Bosman asked for help in interpreting the results of a calculus test, I groaned because I have a black hole in that portion of my brain reserved for math. Jim laughed, then said that he was not asking me to "do" math. He wanted us to review a test he had given to his precalculus students. Jim told us that his observation of his students at work had taught him that kids have a prescribed way of solving problems and learning math. They get stymied easily and only focus on getting the right answer. To address this, Jim had written this test in such a way that students needed to show their work and write about their approach to the problem in order to receive full credit. His question to us, using the Consultancy Protocol outlined in Figure 7.1, was how he could structure the test to receive more consistent responses from students. The Consultancy Protocol is an example of one strategy we use during our CFG meetings.

I realized that by sharing my interpretation of the test questions, I could help Jim with his dilemma. He undoubtedly has someone just like me in his math class, so if I could help him make the task comprehensible to me, he could reach students who processed information in the same way I did.

Jim has also spent time helping me recast my assignments to make them more accessible to students who need information presented in a more linear way. Together, we learn to help each other help students.

When art teacher Liz Gosselin presented her work to our CFG, she showed us slides of cave drawings and played music for us. She then asked us to participate in painting a mural of the drawings we had just seen in the slides. Liz is at the beginning stage of developing her professional development plan. Her questions revolve around how to gather resources, establish a scope and sequence of a curriculum, and vary instruction. By teaching us a lesson she has developed, she invited us to climb into her work with her students. We could begin to understand the questions she has about her work.

Figure 7.1
Consultancy Protocol

Roles: Presenter (whose work is being discussed by the group); facilitator (who also participates)
Time: At least 1 hour

1. Individually, the presenters give a quick overview of their work. They highlight the major issues or problems with which they are struggling, and frame a question for the consultancy group to consider. The framing of this question, as well as the quality of the presenters' reflection on the work and/or issues being discussed, are key features of this protocol. (10 minutes)
2. The consultancy group asks clarifying questions of the presenters—that is, questions that have brief, factual answers. (5 minutes)
3. The group then asks probing questions of the presenters—these questions should be worded so that they help the *presenters clarify* and expand their thinking about the issues and questions they raised for the consultancy group. The goal here is for the presenters to learn more about the question they framed and to do some analysis of the issues they presented. The presenters respond to the group's questions, but there is no discussion by the larger group of the presenters' responses. (10–15 minutes)
4. The group then talks with each other about the work and issues presented. What did we hear? What didn't we hear that we needed to know more about? What do we think about the questions and issues presented? The conversation should include both "warm" and "cool" comments. The presenters are not allowed to speak during this discussion, but instead listen and take notes. (15 minutes)

5. The presenters then respond to what they heard (first in a fishbowl if there are several presenters). A whole group discussion might then take place, depending on the time allotted. (10–15 minutes)
6. The facilitator leads a brief conversation about the group's observations of the process. (5–10 minutes)

(Developed as part of the Coalition of Essential Schools' National Re:Learning Faculty Program and further adapted and revised as part of the work by Annenberg Institute's National School Reform Faculty Project.)

When I bring a piece of curriculum to my CFG and express my doubts about the work, they "tune in" to help me improve it. When I have a classroom dilemma that I can't sort through, my CFG serves as consultants, offering perspectives of the problem that I cannot see from the inside. When I want to see what my students are learning as opposed to what I am teaching, I bring student work to the CFG table and ask my colleagues to tell me what they see. And so, I learn.

I have learned the value of bringing work-in-progress to my CFG, knowing that their questions will challenge my thinking. They will join me in making my work the best that it can possibly be to meet my students' needs. This gift of time and shared purpose exists only in CFG.

ACTIVE PARTICIPANTS IN A LEARNING COMMUNITY

As a member and facilitator of a Critical Friends Group, I become part of a national conversation about the state of our schools. Through the work of this organization, I have received training in professional portfolios, observation and debriefing, and examining student work. I have been asked to share my experiences with other teachers throughout the country.

Our membership in a Critical Friends Group underscores a belief that we should be active participants of a community of learners. We each belong to many rings of membership at our high school, but none of them focuses exclusively on adult learning. Our Critical Friends Groups are the only place in school specifically designed to focus on each of us as a learner, and it is that sustained focus that improves our work.

Some of us use our CFG groups as support for research we want to conduct as a result of questions we raise in our work. For example, one of my colleagues spent several years mastering complex software in order to help students understand the relationship between natural resources and land use planning; another analyzed the relationship between his professional development activities and student learning. Two teachers developed interactive web sites; another mastered digital technology for use in his photography classes. My own research evolved into a book, *Standards of Mind and Heart: Creating the Good High School*. As part of our own school's professional development plan, teachers who conduct a sustained focus on questions of inquiry present their research to a public audience of administrators, board members, and peers. Each of us relied on the support and expertise of our CFG colleagues to help us revise and refine our research, and to prepare for this public presentation.

In her writing, Linda Darling-Hammond (2000) underscores the necessity of building strong links between professional development and student learning. She states the understanding that teachers need extensive learning opportunities:

> So that the complex practices envisioned by ambitious standards have a chance to be studied, debated, tried out, analyzed, retried, and refined until they are well-understood and incorporated into the repertoire of those who teach and make decisions in schools. These opportunities must be collaborative rather than individualistic. (p. 223)

Our Critical Friends Groups allow us to explore these complex practices in a collegial, collaborative environment. CFGs provide a public forum for our questions, reflections, analysis, feedback, and new learning—an extremely valuable structure that links adult learning to improved student achievement.

REFERENCES

Darling-Hammond, L. (2000). *The right to learn: A blueprint for creating schools that work*. San Francisco: Jossey-Bass.

Silva, P., & Mackin, R. A. (2002). *Standards of mind and heart: Creating the good high school*. New York: Teachers College Press.

CHAPTER 8

All Together Now: Reflection as a Community Activity

Simon Hole

I have known for some time that examining student work is a doorway into collegial reflective practice, and my years of working with Educators Writing for Change have strengthened this belief. When we come together to share our writing, we puzzle over not only the writing itself but also the meaning behind the words. As colleagues, we affect each other's practice every time we do so.

The inclusion of parents in the process of examining student work—a priority set by our school improvement team—has given me more to reflect on and was the genesis of this chapter.

As teachers, we strive to create classroom environments in which our students will thrive, places where learning and growth are the norm. We do our best to provide rich experiences and ample opportunities for reflection. We ask our students to work together and we help them learn the requisite group process skills. And, when everything comes together, when the students are flourishing in a strong, nurturing community of learners, we sometimes find ourselves wondering, "What will happen to these kids next year? Is this the norm for our school?"

So we work within our schools, building collegial relationships and learning how to work together. We take the time to establish open and effective communication and develop processes for examining tough issues. We reflect together, asking ourselves what we want our students to know and be like, what our common expectations should be and how we might work toward them. And, when everything comes together, when the staff is flourishing in a strong, nurturing community of learners, we sometimes find ourselves wondering,

"What happens with these kids when they are not in school? Is this the norm for our community?"

So we turn to the task of widening our reach to include parents and others interested in the education of our children. We search for ways to bring them into the conversation, to widen the circle that is our community of learners. In the elementary school where I teach, this has included inviting parents to sessions designed to define quality writing. Although willing to help, some parents felt conflicted about taking on this new role:

> When I first read the notice concerning this workshop, I was conflicted. As a parent, I felt I should attend. I was intrigued by the idea of parents and teachers working together to create a definition of quality student work. But it's always been hard for me to come into schools. I know they don't mean to, but teachers and principals often make me feel as if I'm inadequate. So when I first sat down here tonight, what I felt was fear. (*Anna Botinelli, parent*)

Rhode Island state law requires that every school form a School Improvement Team composed of parents, teachers, and administrators. A key task for this group is the creation of a plan designed to improve student learning. In my school, the School Improvement Team established the examination of student work as one of several priorities. One goal states, "Parents and other community members will be invited to participate in the examination of student work in order to set standards, define quality, and establish benchmarks."

Once the plan is formulated, Action Teams, also composed of parents, teachers, and administrators, are formed and charged with implementing the goals. Those of us on the Action Team responsible for examining student work recognized an opportunity to expand our learning community beyond the school. With this in mind, we set out to design an evening that would bring parents and teachers together.

> When we first started planning, we struggled with the question of how we would present ourselves to the parents. We knew it would be important to create a level playing field—a place where everybody's ideas would be heard and considered. We wanted the participants to feel comfortable enough to engage

in thoughtful conversation. We needed to dispel the myth that we are somehow the experts and that it is our job to provide all the answers to all the questions. In terms of the children, the parents are the experts. (*Sharon Sensiba, teacher*)

All of us on the committee have experience with the "expert syndrome" of which Sharon was speaking. We know that expertise is "primarily a sociological phenomenon [which] concerns human relations and moral and civic responsibilities as much as it does the accumulation of technical knowledge and skill" (Welker, 1992, p. 1). And we know that being viewed as experts often gets in the way of meaningful dialogue.

So it was difficult for us. We are experts in the sense that we have acquired a certain amount of knowledge and skill. What we needed to do was find a way to leverage that expertise, to use it in a way that wouldn't "put off" the parents. We decided that our expertise is about teaching, not about content. We wouldn't pretend to know what the standards and benchmarks should be. But we would use our teaching expertise to design a workshop that would allow a group of parents and teachers to begin that work while also expanding our community of learners. (*Paul Contrell, teacher*)

The team chose to begin with student writing and asked all seven fourth-grade classrooms to provide us with three samples from students representing a cross section of ability levels. We scheduled the library for 6:30–8:00 on a Tuesday evening. We secured the sponsorship of the PTO and wrote a letter of invitation, copies of which went home with every student in the school and were distributed to the staff.

From the beginning, we were worried about whether or not anyone would come. While our PTO is very supportive and does much good work within the school, attendance at their meetings is always very low. This kind of thing just hadn't been done, and nobody knew what to expect. Besides, it was May and we were competing with sports and all sorts of other after-school activities. We were all very relieved when nearly 40 people responded to our invitation. (*Simon Hole, teacher*)

The plan we created was both simple and complex. We wanted the participants, both parents and teachers, to look at a variety of student writings and talk about what they saw. Those of us on the team who had previous experience with examining student work believed that from these conversations, a sense of what constitutes quality writing would emerge.

> We kicked around several ideas, but settled on this particular plan because it felt comfortable. This is something my partner and I do all the time in our classrooms—we have the students look closely at the work the class is doing and they begin to define the characteristics of quality work. I think that is one thing that I will take away from this parent night. I've learned that there isn't much difference between what we do with our students and what we should be doing with adults. (*Lois Morris, teacher*)

The complexity began with the time frame—we would have only an hour and a half. The trick would be to strike a balance between getting through the work of the night and creating a reflective environment. We knew that educational jargon often got in the way of conversations with parents, so we created a list of vocabulary words, defining terms that we felt would be useful. Although group norms are best if created by the group during their first meeting, the time limitation dictated that we post a set of norms, explain what they were about, and ask if anyone had anything to add to the list.

> We knew that the first ten minutes would be crucial. We wanted to get through the introductions, our history of examining student work, set the purpose for the evening, and get through the vocabulary and group norms. All that—and establish an atmosphere conducive to thoughtful reflection! Simon was facilitating and you could tell he was nervous and stumbled a bit at the beginning, but it actually worked okay. People were nodding and smiling by the time we were ready to get started. (*Paul Contrell, teacher*)

Experience told us that it would be easy to get sidetracked, and so we devised a highly structured form, a matrix that would allow us to stay focused on the work at hand. The plan was to pass out the matrix (see Figure 8.1) and a page providing definitions for these characteristics (see Figure 8.2). While most of the definitions were fairly straightforward, we knew that "audience" would be a hard one. Rather than try to "get it right," we chose to let everyone know that it was somewhat ambiguous and have everyone help refine it.

> I knew people would have a lot of questions about this piece, and so rather than spending a lot of time on it, I asked if we could just try using it on the first sample of writing and we'd have time to ask the questions later. So we passed out the sample, everyone found a partner, and they started. It was interesting to watch them begin. The room got so quiet for a while. Then the pairs started sharing their thoughts. I walked from group to group, looking over their shoulders. People asked questions about the writing sample, especially about the level of the student who had written it. Others questioned the categories and definitions, and began to think about how they might be revised. I asked them to bring the questions to the large group. (*Simon Hole, teacher*)

As the groups finished their work, they were asked to share their opinions by placing post-its on a giant version of the continuum that covered a portable blackboard. Most of them ended up in the "shows mastery" or "beyond expectations" columns, but one, in the "audience" category, was placed between "no evidence" and "emerging." It was a very good piece of writing, and when that lone dissenting post-it took its place, there was an audible gasp from the group. When everyone had posted and the facilitator opened the floor to comments, the first statement was, "I want to know who put the post-it way down there."

> I was worried when Nina asked that question. It sounded like a "putdown," and I couldn't understand why Simon didn't say something about how we raise questions or tone of voice. As it turned out, the woman who placed the post-it was not "put off" at all. She was questioning the definition of "audience"

Figure 8.1. Defining Quality Work

For each characteristic, mark an X on the continuum. If a characteristic doesn't seem to apply to this particular work sample, leave the continuum blank and make a note in the space below.

Work Sample _____

Characteristics	No evidence of trait	Trait is just beginning to emerge	Trait is present but needs developing	Shows mastery of trait. Quality work	Trait developed beyond expectations
Mechanics	┝---┼---┥				
Structure	┝---┼---┥				
Style	┝---┼---┥				
Content	┝---┼---┥				
Audience	┝---┼---┥				

Use this space for notes. What else do you see in this piece of work that feels important?

Figure 8.2
Characteristics of Quality Writing

1. *Mechanics.* Punctuation, vocabulary, spelling, grammar, capitalization, and paragraphing are used appropriately.
2. *Structure.* Depending upon the purpose, there is a clear sense of opening, middle, and closing. Sentences follow in a logical order.
3. *Style.* Depending on the type of writing, the author's voice is present through the use of poetic language, figurative language (similes, alliteration, etc.), and varied sentence structure. The sentences flow together.
4. *Content.* Depending upon the purpose, the writing stays on topic, demonstrates comprehension, uses examples, identifies cause and effect, compares and contrasts, creates images, or persuades the reader to adopt the writer's point of view.
5. *Audience.* The writing has a clear sense of purpose. The tone of the writing is appropriate to the intended audience.

---

and while she acknowledged that the writing was very good, she didn't feel it met the definition as stated. It was good that that issue was raised, but I was uncomfortable with how it got started. Before we continued on to other topics, I spoke a bit about the group norms and how it helps if we are careful about how we raise questions. (*Sharon Sensiba, teacher*)

The conversation that flowed from the first writing sample was thoughtful and reflective. The participants questioned the continuum and how it worked in a classroom. They talked of how difficult it was to "score" the writing without having prior experience. They wanted to know the context—what the prompt was and whether the author was a top student. When Jean, the timekeeper for the evening, indicated that the group needed to move on to the next activity, the team made a decision to stay together instead of breaking up into groups as planned.

> I think maybe the best thing we did all night was to change the plan. We had originally wanted to break the group up into two or three smaller groups after the initial activity. I was a bit worried when Simon suggested that we stay together and asked us what we thought. He was saying this in front of all the parents. My first thought was that they would think we didn't know what we were doing. But then I realized this could be a plus. We were showing the parents that following a plan isn't the important thing. The work itself is most important. (*Lois Morris, teacher*)

For the next 30 minutes, pairs of participants picked up other writing samples and worked through the continuum. The writing was varied: poems and essays, stories and revised nursery rhymes, character sketches and book reports set in the form of newspaper pages. Most parents were paired with a teacher. Their conversations focused on the writing, but they also talked about children and how they learn. The time flew, and when the facilitator called them back together, there was good-natured groaning. They didn't want to stop.

With the time remaining, we asked the participants to become more reflective, beginning with the question, "What have we learned tonight about the nature of quality work?" Often with new groups, this can be an awkward time, but the participants started right in.

> I think the main thing I've learned is that using standards like this puts a new twist on everything. It's so different from the traditional A's, B's, and C's we see on report cards. I really like the continuum that we used. I'd rather see that than a report card. It would tell me so much more. I look at the report card and see that Derrick got a B– in writing and I don't really know what that means or how to help him improve. With this, I can see what he's doing well and what he needs to work on. (*Thomas Greene, parent*)

I have a daughter just finishing first grade and a son who will start kindergarten in the fall. I came because I wanted to know more about what would be expected of my children and how I might help them. When I read the first piece of writing, I was amazed and a little worried. I couldn't see how Kathleen could ever get to that level, even in three years. It was reassuring to hear others say the same thing, and to have parents with older children talk about how it does happen. I'm looking forward to watching my daughter grow as a writer. (*Mary Sullivan, parent*)

I'm amazed by the difference in abilities that are mixed together in the same classroom. It must be so hard for teachers to have kids writing at so many different levels. I've always respected teachers, but now . . . I'd love to talk to some of you sometime about how you manage to keep all of your students going. (*Jane Anderson, parent*)

I must admit that I didn't even read the paper announcing tonight's session when my daughter brought it home. It got set aside and if my husband hadn't seen it and pointed it out to me, I wouldn't be here now. I'm glad he saw it. My experience with school meetings has been that someone either wants you to bake or tell you how things should be done. This was very different. I hope these kinds of sessions continue next year. (*Jaleen Blake, parent*)

I'd like the parents to know that we teachers were also feeling a bit nervous about tonight, or at least I was. I really didn't know how this would go. Although we do this kind of work with your children, it felt very risky to get in front of parents and admit that we don't have all the answers. It was very reassuring to see all of you here, thinking hard, and willing to work with us. This is very important work we've started. I'm looking forward to continuing it. (*Lois Morris, teacher*)

The next morning the Action Team met before school to debrief the meeting. As a group, we decided that it would have been better to start with an average piece of writing. The high quality of the first sample may have created a false standard for people, making it difficult to evaluate the other pieces of work. We also agreed that we had to make sure this work continues next year. At the end of the meeting, every parent provided us with a phone number so they could receive special invitations to the next session.

In addition to discussing what we thought went well and what we would change next time, the team members shared their thoughts concerning what they were taking away from the session.

> I've learned over the years that in my classroom, I don't have to be an expert on everything. If I don't know an answer, I can tell the kids, "Let's find that out together." Last night taught me that we can do the same thing with parents. And just saying that now makes me think it must be true in other places as well. Wouldn't it be great if everyone started working together to find answers? (*Sharon Sensiba, teacher*)

> I'm thinking about how hard it can be to meet with parents, but how comfortable last night felt. I mean, this was hard work, but it felt like we were all working together. I wonder if that has to do with the fact that we weren't focusing on individual students. The parents I worked with, they were a couple, and they kept talking about the writing their son brings home. Because the son wasn't in my classroom, I didn't feel as if I had to justify anything or even explain anything. In so many parent interactions, I feel as if the child is somehow standing between us, getting in the way of effective communication. Now I'm thinking about how I might do parent conferences differently—how I might sit next to the parent instead of across from her, and how we might keep the student beside us instead of between us. (*Lois Morris, teacher*)

There is some truth to the saying, "It takes a village to raise a child." But there is a hidden danger when we say the words without really considering what they mean. The saying falls apart if the village is primarily made up of people who want to tell others how things should be. But if the people of the village come together to engage in thoughtful, reflective conversations, if we work together to decide what it is we want for our children, then the saying works. And it could perhaps better be said as, "It takes a community of learners to raise a child."

Including parents in the process of examining student work is valuable on many levels. Students benefit when parents and teachers share a common sense of what constitutes quality work. Teachers gain new insights into their own practice. Parents see that their voices are valued. The culture of the school community, so often isolationist in nature, becomes more inclusive.

And so we work at including all interested parties in the conversations. We enlist their aid in reflecting on what it is we are doing. We find ways to get around the "expert syndrome." We learn to listen hard to each other and to take risks together. And perhaps, when everything comes together, when the students and teachers and parents are all flourishing in a strong, nurturing community of learners, perhaps then we will find something else to wonder about.

REFERENCE

Welker, R. (1992). *The teacher as expert: A theoretical and historical examination.* New York: State University of New York Press.

CHAPTER 9

New Territories

JAN GRANT

Students, faculty, and the community in Narragansett, Rhode Island work together to create and implement school improvement plans. In our ongoing quest to understand and develop new ideas for school reform, collaboration with college and university teacher preparation programs is one project on a long list of goals and objectives.

A colleague's request brought that project to the top of the list. She asked me to fulfill the duties of "peer observer" for her student teacher. As we became involved with this partnership, my colleague, her student teacher, and I explored new territories of reflective practice.

When does the desire to improve our teaching practice strongly permeate our careers? How does one get to a point where the analysis of one's work becomes feasible? Who is responsible for that inquiry? By what method does one introduce the possibility of new ideas to good teachers? When is good, good enough? These are the questions I wondered about as I began to work with Peter, a student teacher in our school district.

I remember Peter Hansen as an older student who came to the United States from Holland to earn a graduate degree in education. He was assigned to our rural high school for his student teaching in physics. Beatrice Hartley, the chairperson of the science department, was his cooperating teacher. Beatrice asked if I would be the outside observer required by the education department of his college. The college required that I observe three classes, discuss the observations with the student teacher, and complete evaluation forms at the end of the semester. Beatrice explained to me that the possibility existed for us to enhance Peter's classroom experience by including deeper analysis and inquiry into teaching and learning with this student teacher.

Our decision to refine the arrangement required by the college changed a simple project into an absorbing experience in professional development and student reflection.

During our first meeting, Beatrice, Peter, and I met in a science classroom where we sat on stools around a black lab table. This meeting provided Peter with an opportunity to state his beliefs at the very beginning of a career in teaching. He said:

> I want to contribute to the community by working with young people. Because I believe the study of science to be useful and exciting, I have decided to develop a career in high school education. I think I can relate to the students because I am a student myself. I hope I have something to offer—I want to learn.

Beatrice introduced me as the "coach" of the high school's Critical Friends Group (CFG). She explained to Peter that Critical Friends Groups are professional learning communities where educators meet regularly in a supportive and challenging environment to improve teaching and learning. My job as coach was to facilitate and lead these bimonthly conversations. Beatrice, a member of our CFG, was a fervent convert to the new procedures and protocols introduced to Critical Friends for the exploration, development, and practice of teaching.

During our first meeting with Peter, Beatrice explained the advantages of open dialogue among colleagues. She felt that frequent, focused conversations led to diminishing the state of isolation felt by teachers in a traditional setting. Peter was attentive but his eyes and body language revealed a slight disinclination to enter unexplored territory. When he leaned forward to speak, his voice was steady and confident as he said:

> My university experiences have made me aware of a number of educational reform movements. I believe they have merit. I also believe in the proven, traditional methods of teaching. They work for me. I will work hard to be a good teacher.

Peter outlined his plan for the lesson that I would be watching the next day. He had been diligent in creating each step. He stood to draw our attention to the chart he had created to demonstrate gravitational force. I thought ahead to the checklist that I was to fill out after his lesson. As the outside observer, the categories that I was instructed to "evaluate" included preparedness, organization, the ability to handle student questions, and clarity of delivery. This meeting was the first opportunity to introduce the possibility of our working toward a different set of goals. I hoped that the suggestion to delve a bit further into his practice would pique Peter's curiosity.

As Peter's presentation and feedback session finished, there was a pause. I saw Beatrice lean back and wait patiently to see how the new approach would take shape. I asked Peter if he would be willing to consider additional challenges to the format proposed by his college. I explained that if he agreed, we would start with a conversation about his goals for teaching. The deliberate pause before he nodded slowly indicated his uncertainty.

I began by asking Peter to identify one educational goal about which he felt passionate. Was there a single accomplishment that he hoped to achieve in his new career in order to feel successful—one achievement that would make teaching worthwhile?

Peter mulled this over while he underlined his notes. After a few minutes, his thoughtful expression changed to one of interest. He looked up and said:

> If I could motivate an excitement in my students so they would ask questions or make connections to take them deeper into the subject matter, I would be very happy. I would like them to become original thinkers so that deeply inquisitive class discussions are regular occurrences.

FIRST OBSERVATION

For my first observation, I sat at a lab table in the back corner of the classroom. The student desks were arranged in rows facing the front of the room. From the outset of this class on gravity, I saw that Peter loved his subject. He conveyed controlled enthusiasm during his well-prepared lesson. He was knowledgeable about his subject matter and easily handled questions from the students. I found myself smiling often, taking pleasure in the knowledge that I was watching a new teacher who enjoyed his work.

After the lecture explaining that the force due to gravity is strongest nearer the center of the earth, Peter instructed the students to work in small groups around the room. Their assignment was to demonstrate an understanding of the lesson through illustration. Lisa was bent over her illustration when, eyes sparkling, her head snapped up. She called out a "discovery" and a question:

> Mr. Hansen! So, in your talk about the force of gravity, you said that its force affects all molecules. Right? Right. So, air molecules are affected by the pull of gravity, too, just like rocks! Air is not really "thin" at all— that must be why so many climbers need to use bottled oxygen on Mount Everest. Cool! Less air molecules are up there—away from the center of gravity! That's it. Isn't that right?!

Peter rushed to her table and enthusiastically called the attention of the class to the example. It seemed that his wish for connection and association occurred for the first time in this very class—apparently an unexpected bonus.

DEBRIEFING

Directly after his lesson, Peter and I walked with Beatrice to an empty room to discuss what had occurred. Peter was amused that we referred to this time as a "debrief." He explained that he had heard the term only in relation to astronauts returning from space expeditions.

We had suggested that he prepare focus questions upon which our debrief session would be based. He asked:

- Were my explanations and answers to questions clear?
- Were the students engaged?
- Was the transition smooth from the lecture mode to the group work at the lab tables?

We had also prepared our own list of debriefing questions listed in Figure 9.1.

After a relaxed conversation about his focus questions, we discussed the "discovery" incident that seemed to meet Peter's objective to motivate curiosity in his students. A young woman made a connection between information in the teacher's lecture and her "discovery"

Figure 9.1
Debriefing Questions

- What did you observe that was unique?
- What did you hear that was thought provoking?
- What did you learn that you might use elsewhere?
- What other connections did you formulate?

---

while drawing an illustration. He was obviously delighted to have achieved a goal that he had so recently voiced.

We asked him to explain why he thought the student had chosen to come up with an analogy about the work. What could he do to ensure that this type of student inquiry would occur on a regular basis? Peter answered immediately. He said:

> I think today was a result of luck—a serendipitous moment. I believe "Eureka" moments happen as a result of the students and their innate abilities. I'm not sure these moments can be planned.

The three of us engaged in a brief conversation on the value of including planned motivation by the teacher to achieve a desired objective in our lessons. Although Peter took an active part in the discussion, he seemed puzzled and a little detached. His focus questions had been answered to his satisfaction. We asked if Peter thought there might be more that he could achieve in the time he was with his students. As I watched him, I wondered again that if by adding a different approach we were overstepping our bounds. I knew, however, that we had begun the type of probing dialogue that Beatrice had anticipated. We were hoping that Peter would enter a new territory in the learning process. How could we encourage him to venture further into the ambiguity of an unknown? We began a second feedback session for deeper reflection on the lesson that had occurred.

We talked about risk-taking and the uncertainty of new methods. We hoped he would understand that the questions in feedback sessions were meant to act as stimuli to provoke deeper reflection about teaching and learning. We were gently prodding him to leave familiar landmarks.

RESPONSE

A weekend passed and on Monday I found Peter's reflection in my mailbox:

> I was disappointed that the kids did not discuss the work within their groups with one another. I assumed they would share their illustrations—learn from each other. I thought about your asking me if I had taught them how to do this. Now, I realize that I had not prepared them for this expectation. I am thinking about the importance of using motivational techniques and teaching skills that fall outside the content area.

The process of Peter's learning to accept different methods for teaching and reflection was exciting to observe. He was an older student. At his university, he had been studying with people whom he admired and respected. He had gained valuable experience in the traditional format of a single teacher working alone with students in a classroom.

The meeting prior to my second observation took a slightly different path. Beatrice had frequently observed my teaching students how to engage in successful dialogue through communication skills development. She stepped onto a "skinny branch" when she suggested that I teach a couple of lessons in Peter's class to demonstrate alternative teaching strategies. When she proposed my visiting more often than was required by his college, Peter listened quietly. Beatrice's suggestion for me to teach in the physics classroom seemed a major leap in collegial trust. In addition, Beatrice recommended that Peter experience the use of protocols—structured procedures—for Peter and me to talk about the teaching he observed. Our roles would be reversed—he would be giving me feedback.

As Peter listened, he sat very still. His attention indicated respect for his cooperating teacher. Peter recognized Beatrice's support of my work, but he seemed unsure of this new territory. Beatrice explained that he would be observing different methods to consider for the development of his teaching practice. I wondered if he understood the risks that even an experienced teacher takes when opting for observation by her colleagues.

I witnessed his struggle to formulate a response to the idea. The muscle in his jaw tightened. Beatrice sat at the end of the table, observing. *She is good at the silent moments,* I thought. He looked directly into my eyes while he thought about what to say. After a long pause Peter spoke in a well-mannered, constrained voice:

> How long will you take away from my class? Maybe the kids would be unwilling to listen to different methods. How will they be able to use this in the future? Will I have time to teach everything that is required for this semester if some class time is taken away?

Beatrice was patient and, as always, positive. She answered his questions calmly. He appeared somewhat convinced. It was decided that I could "have" three 30-minute sessions with his physics class of juniors and seniors for this experiment.

EXPLORATION

I was apprehensive when I entered Peter's classroom to teach my first lesson. It was my objective to stimulate open communication among the students—attempting to create a reflective, nonjudgmental atmosphere for teaching and learning. I believe that this skill needs to be explicitly demonstrated and practiced by students. Time was a constraint and it was challenging to introduce a new element into an established curriculum. My biggest concern, however, was that teaching this skill required a significant investment of time—moving from low-risk activities to ones that required a greater personal challenge. My previous experiences with this method were with students who participated in the process for an entire semester, in an after-school workshop, without the demanding bells that restricted class periods to 45 minutes. This would be a reality check for me.

As my lesson began, I wondered how the students would react to a visiting teacher attempting a new kind of lesson in their science class. It is difficult for students to participate freely when they are asked to share opinions in a class discussion. Typical student concerns are:

Will I say something "stupid"?
Is it "cool" to participate in class?
What does this stuff have to do with class anyway?
Supposing I get "it" wrong?

Peer Observation

I did not have the complete attention of the students at the outset. I explained that I was there to document their opinions on a few everyday topics that might seem unrelated to physics, and that it was perfectly acceptable not to know the information ahead of time—there were no "right" answers. Some of the kids perked up. I told them that their cooperation was important for an experiment in education to see how we could make it better for kids. I explained that our first task was merely to get people comfortable with speaking in class. I asked for opinions about cars, jobs, "wish lists," extracurricular activities, and travel—simple, low-risk, nonthreatening topics.

I called on several students who had not contributed to class discussions previously. Peter had identified a few as "troublesome." Some of those students began by "grandstanding"—but they were participating. The class as a whole became involved when they decided that their opinions mattered to the conversation—however simple the topic. We used an activity called a "Rapid Round," a procedure that took place in a circle format where tightly timed responses were required. As the rounds continued, the significance of the topics amplified and the level of risk increased. (See Figure 9.2 for the steps involved in a Rapid Round.)

I asked them to find the courage to speak in public without knowing the outcome. I explained that Beatrice, Peter, and I would uphold

---

Figure 9.2
Rapid Round

1. Present a focus question to a group in a circle.
2. Designate individual answer time.
3. Allow participants to pass.

the group norm of nonjudgment. We would encourage a safe atmosphere for freedom of opinion in the classroom. Negative peer pressure, put-downs, and nonverbal negativism would not be appropriate. I taught "I-messaging," a method of communication where the speaker uses only personal pronouns to avoid assumptions about the perspectives of participants. We asked the students to brainstorm a list of expectations that would become the group norms for their class (see Figure 9.3).

In the notes that Beatrice took during the lesson, she wrote:

I noticed unparalleled participation today and I am amazed that these easy process skills have so much in common with our study of science. The kids were involved in an experiment even though they were not sitting at lab tables. They employed logic, exploration, and discovery. They were taking incredible

---

Figure 9.3
Group Norms for Process Work in Grade 11 Physics

1. Give new ideas a chance to succeed.
2. Eliminate put-downs!
3. Develop a respectful attitude.
4. Help all students to be responsible.
5. Accept differences.
6. Say what you mean and mean what you say.
7. Avoid side conversations while others are speaking.
8. Listen actively.
9. Allow ideas to be completed without interruption.
10. Use "I-messages."
11. Be a good example.
12. Display commitment and a seriousness of purpose.
13. Ask questions for a better understanding of this process.
14. Say it in the classroom if you are thinking it.
15. Address infractions to the rules of the classroom and to these group norms.
16. Have fun.

personal risks. That Jean and Derek ever became vocal in these activities floored me. When Joel said, "This is stupid!" I thought, "Uh-oh, here we go." But your reply stimulated that intense discussion of why things that are different seem stupid. We can *use* this! It is a conundrum very evident in the history of science.

Changes

The extent of Peter's willingness to accept the importance of teaching process skills changed gradually. Increased class participation seemed to be the motivation. It was the path to realizing his personal objective of "deeply inquisitive class discussions."

For the second and third demonstration lessons, I used focus questions that had to do with significant school procedures. I explained to the students that their opinions were central to the possibility of changing methods for teaching and learning. The kids became more deeply involved in having their voices heard. Topics about scheduling, teaching methods, length of class time, teacher evaluations by students, and grading systems were included. The risks of public participation tripled. Real answers would bare real feelings. Peer approval was on the line. Students had to think carefully about what was important in order to answer truthfully and seriously. We expected them to speak their own truths. The whole time, our nonjudgmental environment was protected by the clarity of group norms.

As the weeks progressed and the process sessions continued, Peter became increasingly intrigued by the evolving process. Beatrice's "thumbs-up" signals were enthusiastic when we happened to see each other in the crowds passing in the wide school corridors. Peter experienced increased class participation and was careful to honor the group norms that were introduced in the process lessons. His initial goal of escalating inquisitive classroom conversation occurred on several occasions. He discussed the possibility of introducing some of the ideas that he was exploring during his student teaching with his own college classmates. Peter facilitated our increasingly intense rapid-fire feedback sessions illuminated by the following questions:

- Are process lessons worth the time they take away from the subject matter? Are the results measurable?
- How much can be expected from disinterested students? How can we motivate them?

- Is there another way to "reward" excellence in addition to grades?
- How many additions to my personal objectives for my teaching career are reasonable to attain?
- How much extra work is feasible to expect from a teacher? A student?

We were traveling a different terrain and were nearing the end of our time together. Our work to introduce and hone the skill of focused conversations in the classroom had grown and developed throughout the semester. Peter seemed to be gaining a broader perspective on teaching by accepting the use of communication protocols, planned motivation, and collaborative inquiry with his students. During one of our debrief sessions, it was reassuring to hear him say:

I understand the necessity to teach skills that may have nothing to do with physics—what you call "process skills." The workshops in communication, personal awareness, writing, and creating an atmosphere of nonjudgment help the students to learn science.

NOW WHAT?

What more could we learn? As Peter's time at the high school drew to a close, he began to prepare an evaluation form by which the students would assess his student teaching. Our work together led him to an additional possibility.

It was long after the last bell when only an occasional footstep echoed in the empty corridors. From Beatrice's office, we heard the faraway drone of the waxing machines in the cafeteria. The clang of coins and the clunk of a soda can resonated from the teachers' room nearby. The time seemed right to introduce another "less-traveled path" to our exploration.

We explained to Peter the idea of an open forum where students, through a structured protocol, would be invited to comment on his work. There were risks inherent in the project. If he agreed, Peter would hear a critical assessment of his teaching based on a wide range of questions developed by the three of us. Had we taught sufficiently and learned enough to ask the students to join us in this endeavor?

Peter had planned to distribute an evaluation checklist to the students, but he became interested in the exploration of yet another new territory. His slight apprehension was overshadowed by his eagerness to experience the inquiry.

A Training Session

We agreed upon a final opportunity for Peter and his students. We would find an appropriate protocol around which to design and implement a workshop to debrief Peter's teaching with the juniors and seniors who had been working with us all semester. We began our final preparations. At this point, I held two training sessions to prepare students for their involvement in the culminating experience of a Collaborative Assessment Protocol. The training procedure would teach the structure and the expectations of the upcoming protocol. The kids commented on why the training sessions were helpful:

> I felt that I was being trained for a real reason—being taught because it was for something important coming up.
> I really had to know what I was doing to be fair to Mr. Hansen—I had to pay attention in the training.
> I wonder why this training stuff doesn't happen in school more often. We have to learn how to do what we have to do.
> I believe that it matters what I say in here.

The Final Trek

Beatrice managed to arrange an extra 35 minutes for the special session. She reserved a larger, less confining classroom that was furnished with big tables and comfortable chairs. A different, more pleasant environment and special treatment would make the occasion important and motivate the kind of cooperation necessary for a dynamic conversation. When adults attend workshops and special meetings they are given tools and a good working environment. We did the same for our students. Pads, pens, and refreshments were set at each place as at a conference.

As each group of students entered the room, they looked pleased and surprised—even those who were used to exuding boredom. They wandered in, searched the room for the "ideal" place, and slowly found seats.

Quiet and observant, Peter leaned on a bookcase in the corner. I noticed how intense he looked. I wondered how he would respond to student feedback. Was he concerned about the outcome? Would the kids share real opinions? What kinds of honesty and risk-taking would be demonstrated?

The workshop began with an explanation of the Collaborative Assessment Protocol—the procedure that we planned to use to conduct a facilitated conversation. (See Figure 9.4 for a summary of the protocol.)

We needed to hear what students thought. One of the reasons we were there was for all of us to learn. Group norms were about to be tested. Uncensored input was crucial for kids and teachers to find out how to do this "school thing" a little better.

As I walked inside the oval to distribute the focus questions and the agenda outline for our Collaborative Assessment Protocol, a few kids glanced at their teacher. Peter jotted notes in a spiral binder.

The protocol started and the students jumped into the discussion. They were hungry to share. At first we heard hesitant praise and tentative criticism. Some kids looked over to check on Peter's reaction. Soon, leaders emerged who encouraged the more silent students to

---

Figure 9.4
Collaborative Assessment Protocol

1. Facilitator presents work to be discussed.
2. The group reviews the work.
3. Participants provide comments on the work.
4. Facilitator asks for questions that have resulted from examining the work.
5. Facilitated discussion occurs.
6. Presenting teacher offers closing comments.
7. All comment on the implications to teaching and learning.
8. Group reflects together on their experiences or reactions to the procedure.

(Adapted from the Collaborative Assessment Conference Protocol by Steve Seidel and colleagues at Harvard University's Zero Project, 1996.)

contribute—and they did. I watched eyes sparkle as kids leaned toward each other while speaking. Inadvertently, the class used the group norms we had practiced throughout the semester. Topic questions were introduced into the protocol:

- How would you describe the successes in Mr. Hansen's teaching?
- Is there anything you would have done differently?
- What did you learn in addition to physics?
- What rubrics and standards were addressed?
- Were your needs met?
- Are you prepared to have a conversation on the subject of physics?

There were a number of surprises, a great deal of honesty, and much passion. Peter forgot to write for a while to watch this event unfurl. Beatrice was able to bring her attention to her laptop to jot down a few student comments:

I thought some of the process stuff we did at first was stupid, but I know now that we would not be talking today if we didn't do the stupid stuff first. Like, we shouldn't do this kind of workshop if we don't use "I-messages."

Mr. Hansen's teaching was good because it changed. I didn't sit there just listening to speeches all the time.

Sometimes I didn't have enough quiet time to think or to say that I didn't know.

It was good that kids who were mean were called on it.

Mr. Hansen made me interested in physics. Maybe I want to be a teacher.

Sometimes Mr. Hansen thought we already knew what we needed to know for a new lesson—that's not true all the time.

I think it is very important for students to have a voice. Today is a good example of that.

Peter listened carefully. When he responded, his students hung on his every word. He complimented them on their ability to participate freely. I wondered if the students realized how courageous their teacher had been to agree to the personal risks entailed in the workshop. As the kids left, the three of us walked to the door to see them spilling down the hall, forming their groups and still talking. "Don't you just love that," Beatrice commented, "when they leave your room and talk about the *lesson*!"

REFLECTION

A week later, I compiled my observation notes and completed the required forms for mailing to Peter's college. Peter's final reflection illustrated the path he had traveled during our work together. He wrote:

> To have the students take part in a Collaborative Assessment workshop was very informative for me. It engaged the students in the lifelong learning experience of providing feedback. The students answered questions I had about my teaching in a non-critical manner and in a safe environment. By participating in a number of different activities and protocols, the students gained skills that will be useful throughout their academic and adult careers. There is a great deal to think about.

The work that Peter, Beatrice, the students, and I did together provided new learning for all of us. In my mind, that is the goal of authentic classroom experience and assessment—to move from simple certainty to more ambiguous, complex uncertainty, and helpful truths.

CHAPTER 10

More than One Kind of Sandwich: A District Begins a Conversation about Reflective Practice

JoAnne Dowd

In this chapter, I share a story about an experience that led to much learning for me as a person and as a professional, an experience that allowed me to see the bigger picture even as it unfolded.

When I wrote "More than One Kind of Sandwich," I was a high school teacher in rural Maine. This chapter describes the importance of having clear goals before asking teachers to open their practice to colleagues outside of their own school.

Since then, I have become a district-level administrator in another school system. This story has become for me a cautionary tale about how good ideas sometimes get lost through poor implementation. As an administrator, I vowed to remember this lesson learned.

Our school district, comprised of a high school, a middle school, and several elementary schools in rural Maine, had received a sizable grant—$10,000—to encourage reflective practice among teachers. The Libra Foundation, based in Maine, funds educational projects within the state. The goal of the grant was to improve classroom practice. It would provide an opportunity for teachers to look at their work in a focused way apart from the daily frenzy of life in schools. Teachers could see their work through new eyes and with a fresh perspective. Most importantly, the grant would encourage teachers across the district to make their work public.

The Assistant Superintendent decided to begin the grant work with an introductory workshop for all members of the district. The

topic of the workshop would be the "Tuning Protocol," a highly structured format for giving and receiving feedback developed by David
Allen and Joe McDonald, colleagues at the Coalition of Essential
Schools (CES) at Brown University. Our high school faculty had experi-
mented with uses for the protocol over the previous months, and a
small group of us were invited to bring work to be "tuned" to this
opening workshop.

The tuning protocol was just one of a series of reflection activities
being designed by CES and the Annenberg Institute of School Reform
(AISR)(Allen, 1995). We chose it as a starting point because of its
straightforward nature. It was a process that could be learned and
used easily—an adaptable tool that could be used in a variety of
situations. It was an efficient way for practitioners to make focused
use of limited common planning time.

The simplicity and clarity of the tuning protocol make it an ideal
initial approach to reflective practice. Our assistant superintendent
felt that the introduction of the tuning protocol district-wide as a first
exposure to reflective practice would give faculty at least one strategy
that was immediately accessible to them. Since many in our high
school staff were familiar with the concept of reflective practice, and
several had been trained to use the tuning protocol, in his mind, we
were the natural choice to teach and model the protocol, and to usher
in the first, district-wide initiative.

THE TUNING PROTOCOL

In the tuning protocol format, a presenter's lesson plan, along with
the class work resulting from it, gets "tuned" by peers during a lengthy
session. (See Figure 10.1 for a list of the steps involved.) Included
in the process are scheduled times for the presenter to talk about a
work in progress, to answer participants' questions, to get "warm"
(positive) and "cool" (suggestions for improvement) feedback from
the participants, and time to respond to any of the feedback she or
he chooses. A trained peer facilitates the session and ensures that there
is equal time for both speaking and listening, and that the norms for
the protocol are observed. At the end of the session, the entire group
participates in a debriefing of the tuning protocol experience and they
discuss how the protocol would best suit their own needs as educators.

Figure 10.1
Tuning Protocol

1. *Introduction.* Facilitator briefly introduces protocol goals, guidelines, and schedule. Participants briefly introduce themselves. (10 minutes)
2. *Teacher Presentation.* Teacher presents the context for student work (assignment, scoring rubric, etc.) and the focusing question for feedback on it. (20 minutes)
3. *Clarifying Questions.* Facilitator judges which are clarifying questions and which more properly belong in the Warm and Cool Feedback period. (5 minutes maximum)
4. *Examination of Student Work Samples.* Samples of student work might be original or photocopied pieces of written work and/or video clips. (15 minutes)
5. *Pause to Reflect on Warm and Cool Feedback.* Participants may take a couple of minutes to reflect and/or write down what they would like to contribute to the feedback session. (2–3 minutes)
6. *Warm and Cool Feedback.* Participants share feedback while teacher-presenter is silent. Facilitator may remind participants of teacher-presenter's focusing question. (15 minutes)
7. *Reflection.* Teacher-presenter speaks to those comments/questions he or she chooses to, while participants are silent. Facilitator may intervene to focus, clarify, etc. (15 minutes)
8. *Debriefing.* Participants discuss the "tuning experience" that they have shared. (10 minutes)

His intention was to provide training for everyone, so that faculty at each school would have a common vocabulary and a common experience with which to begin our work. A District Reflective Practice Group was formed through the appointment of two "coaches" at each school. These coaches' role was to encourage teachers in their buildings to work toward the goal of the grant—to become reflective practitioners and to encourage reflective practice among their peers. They would also come together monthly to share ideas, successes, and challenges, and to bring information and ideas back to their individual buildings.

Preparation

Throughout my preparation time in the days before the workshop, I felt fairly confident that the presentation would go well. I planned to present a series of recently developed lessons tying art and literature together. Since it was the first time I had consciously made an effort to tie art so explicitly into my work as an English teacher, I had some questions. I was excited about the prospect of getting some feedback on how to make my lessons more challenging and fully developed.

The project was a children's book that students had created together, with one student writing text and another illustrating. I had two questions: Could an observer tell whether the child who had created the illustrations understood the literature? Was this a valid assessment for both the student doing the writing and the one doing the artwork?

PRESENTATION DAY

Sitting at a table, in a noisy cafeteria that doubled as an auditorium, with my styrofoam cup of bad coffee and stale danish in hand, I suddenly realized the magnitude of what I was about to do. In just a few moments, at the end of the droning keynote address, I would open up *my* classroom to colleagues, who knew little or nothing of me or the context of my school. And, so that groups participating in the protocol could remain small, we had been asked to repeat our presentation three times.

An Unexpected Response

The response of the first audience could be characterized by the question, "Is this something we are going to have to do at every meeting from now on?" This group translated my presentation as *the way* to be reflective. They assumed that my demonstration of a particular technique meant they would be required to incorporate it immediately into their daily lives. Some really hit the panic button. They were filled with questions that I, as a presenter, really couldn't answer for them, such as, "How often do we have to do these tuning things?" and, "Will this mean we have to go to more meetings now?"

Their anxiety may have been the result of working in a school that did not foster an atmosphere of positive experimentation where teachers are free to try a variety of approaches, modifying, rejecting or changing them as necessary. No one had explained to them, or they didn't or couldn't hear, that this was just one tool—one possible way of approaching reflective practice. They viewed it as "the thing" rather than "a tool to help build 'the thing.'" They did not know that the district had plans to empower several teachers from each building to lead study groups of different types, based on the interests and culture of each school throughout the district. Maybe their administrators had not presented this as an option. Even if the "option" had been offered, perhaps, because of past experiences, they hadn't believed it would really happen. Perhaps their panic and frustration were justified. Perhaps not.

A Moment of Discouragement

The second group, in contrast, could be characterized by the following: *"This word is grammatically incorrect. Isn't this an English classroom?"* The members of the second workshop simply refused to participate in the tuning. One colleague sat with his back toward me, twirling a pencil and chatting with the person sitting next to him for the entire presentation. To be successful, the protocol requires participation from all those at the table.

When it was time for the feedback-giving session, the participants stared blankly at me or looked down at the table. Finally, one woman spoke up, noting a grammatical error on one of the student-designed rubrics I had distributed earlier. She wanted to know why there was such an error in an English classroom. I explained to her that the students had designed and created the rubric. I wanted to honor their work and keep it as much theirs as possible, considering that it was their first attempt at creating a rubric. She harrumphed and became silent. No further comments ensued.

After an agonizing session, this group left me, and we had a break for lunch. I realized how blithely I had earlier underestimated the impact of this experience. When I had first agreed to participate, one of five volunteers giving a presentation to peers, I considered it a simple activity. This simple activity revealed itself as something a lot more complicated. The issues being communicated to me—distrust, fear, judgment—I had never thought possible considering the professional culture in my own building.

This was the first time I had been given the opportunity to look beyond my own building to realize that I was connected to other people in the district. I didn't necessarily like what was happening to me that day, but I was already in the middle of it. I began to wonder what could be changed and improved in the future so we could improve the quality of the dialogue around the district. I made a decision to get more involved in the District Reflective Practice Group, a volunteer group consisting of one or two representatives from each of the eight schools that came together monthly to share ideas and experiences. Each of these volunteers served as a reflective practice coach in his or her school and led the faculty in a series of activities. Even though this had been an uncomfortable experience so far, I could see the potential good that could come from breaking down the barriers created by years of lack of communication and misperceptions across the district. After all, we were all on the same team, and all wanted the best for our students. Didn't it make sense to find a way to work together on behalf of our collective students?

A Change in Tone

My workshop after lunch was a success. One participant exclaimed, "I'm moving to this district and putting my children in your classroom if this is the kind of thing going on there." Another said, "We hear so many negative things going on at the high school. It's nice to talk to someone who is actually there to see what's happening."

In addition, there were several art and music teachers in the group who felt validated by being asked, for the first time ever, their opinion on a professional release day. I wondered how often we've ignored experts in our presence as we've rushed out to find "experts" else-where to teach us.

Upon reflection, it quickly became obvious that each group of teachers who attended the tuning protocol workshop arrived with a different understanding of the workshop's purpose. One teacher who participated in the experience commented on her reflection sheet:

> We were introduced to the idea of reflective practice as if the tuning protocol was the only way to be reflective. It would be like taking a peanut butter and jelly sandwich to a six-year old saying, "This is a sandwich," so that the child would be left thinking, "This is the only kind of sandwich that exists," in-stead of introducing it by saying, "This is a peanut butter and jelly sandwich. It's only one kind of sandwich. You can also have a turkey sandwich, bologna, avocado, and cheese."

Faculty from schools attending the presentation brought percep-tions from previous experiences with staff development. They came with preconceived notions about the high school and its teachers—concerns about the Coalition of Essential Schools based on second-hand information. We probably should have begun the day by addressing their misperceptions. Their frame for receiving new information was probably quite small.

I pondered the role of the district, as well as my role as a teacher in professional development. It seemed important for our work to be pushed, but equally important to model the very practices the district office were asking of their employees across the district. In hindsight, the whole experience has led me to think about what might have been done differently, right from the start, to get more people involved with and excited about examining their work in a new way. The assistant superintendent could have worked with the building admin-istrators to make sure everyone had a clear picture of the day and were reminded to share this information in a consistent way with their staffs. Some level of trust needed to be built across the district before asking teachers to put their work on display.

Teachers from all levels could have been included in the planning process. Then the tone of the day, and of the year, could have been entirely different. When people have a say—in this case, a say in their own development as teachers—exciting and meaningful things are more likely to happen. We know this about the students in our classrooms. As adult learners, we tend to forget it about ourselves. I wondered how different the experience would have looked and felt if a team of faculty from all the buildings had come together and planned the districtwide staff development day. They may or may not have chosen the exact same activity, but the way in which it was received would have been radically different.

In reality, every school does not consist of faculty who work on interdisciplinary teams, who share ideas and critique each other's work, and who freely engage in a whole range of decision making from curriculum to use of time. Just as my ideas about teaching and staff development were tied to the particular culture at my school, every other person's in that district was tied to his or hers.

As a result, many staff members from schools across the district heard "This is a sandwich" about the tuning protocol as opposed to "this is only one kind of sandwich." We in the District Reflective Practice Group spent the whole year trying to overcome this initial mindset. Even at the end of the year, despite many discussions to the contrary, there were reflective practice coaches at other schools who still thought of the tuning protocol as *the way* and not as *one way* of accomplishing our goals.

Still, I am encouraged that across the district a dialogue about reflective practice had begun. As coaches on equal footing, we came together once a month to share ideas and challenges as a way of collaborating. We developed our own agenda—together. No one was being force-fed a certain kind of "sandwich." We hoped that those meetings would allow reflective practice in all its forms to spread across the district. In addition, as this dialogue allows for the circulation of ideas at each school, individuals may become empowered to have a voice in their own future staff development.

I developed a new appreciation for the culture at my school. I felt confident that the ideas I brought to my peers from colleagues elsewhere in the district would be considered and given a trial run. I now have a heightened awareness of the complexity of school reform, not only within a school but also across a district. Sometimes even potentially valuable and well-intentioned school reform initiatives can backfire. We need to proceed with tolerance and patience—and then take the forward leap together.

REFERENCE

Allen, D. (1995, February). *The tuning protocol: A process for reflection*. Studies on Exhibitions, no. 15. Providence, RI: Coalition of Essential Schools.

CHAPTER 11

Growing Reflective Practitioners

GRACE HALL MCENTEE

We have come full circle. This final chapter returns to the beginning of Educators Writing for Change. Here we gather to think about, write, and revisit teaching events—the same process that brought us together.

"We are teachers," we say, "not writers." As we continue to learn and grow through sharing our writing with others, we realize that this process intensifies reflection. We scrutinize our practice and worry over the nuance of words that describe it. We learn to listen to those who read what we have written, those who come with fresh questions and surprising insights.

We are akin to caterpillars, all of us. At some critical moment through our own willpower or through the assistance of others we can enter a chrysalis, evolve through an amorphous state, and emerge changed. When practitioners came to a retreat to write about practice with Joe Check and me, some were able to do that. They moved through a period of writing just to write and of sharing just to share. When they emerged from the cocoon of the retreat (see Figure 11.1) and returned to their schools and classrooms, some felt different. From this first step of a yearlong process intended to nurture education practitioner-writers for publication, they had emerged like delicate butterflies. As evolving reflective practitioners they flew in startling hues and in all of their fragility back to schools, which more often than not are the antithesis of a field of flowers.

The retreat was drawing to a close. We joined in a circle for a final go-round, each taking thirty seconds to give some last thought concerning the work we had done over the past three days. By chance of seating, I was near the end of the group.

Figure 11.1
Mini-retreats

Monthly meetings of colleagues—mini-retreats—could serve the same purpose as a weekend retreat detailed within this narrative. At these mini-retreats in school or at the home of a colleague, practitioners can in the same way learn to share and reflect upon written stories from their practice.

When my turn came, I stood, and, as if at an AA meeting, proclaimed, "My name is Simon, and I am a writer." (*Simon Hole*)

Simon was a practitioner who had written during his university years and, in a different way, as a teacher preparing assignments for his fourth-grade class. This, however, was the first time he had deliberately written about his teaching practice and risked going public with that writing.

Over time, Joe and I, Simon, and other participants have stayed with the process. We have found that writing about practice means traveling backwards to the school or classroom, going beyond the moment to discover what else it holds. Upon further reflection an incident becomes larger than itself:

The difficulty in writing for me isn't to find stories to tell; teaching is a profession that generates stories. Instead, it is to create narratives and understand teaching in a larger sense, in the context of my life, my school, my community, and all the debates and issues surrounding education. (*Steve Dreher*)

In the next section I will describe the process through which we—facilitators and writers—found our way from writing to reflective practice, from thinking about what we say as writers to thinking about what we do as practitioners. It sounds like a process that puts the cart before the horse and, indeed, reflection is a backwards or recursive process.

I was on leave from teaching and working at the Coalition of Essential Schools (CES) at Brown University. One day I showed Ted Sizer—founder and director of CES—some writing I had done about my teaching practice. "Would this have any value in our work?" I said.

"Why don't you gather writers from around the country and use your writing as a catalyst," he said. I didn't know exactly what that meant, but as I left his office I knew his words had launched me into a new zone of learning, like none I had experienced in my adult life.

Joe Check, director of the Boston Writing Project, had consulted with Brown University for another project—The Teacher's Journal—that involved other teacher writers and me. Through funding, by CES and later by the Annenberg Institute for School Reform (AISR), we built upon the process we had previously used with that publication. We designed a yearlong experience for a group of 30 practitioners. For each of 2 years, a writers' conference kicked off the process, which provided professional support for participants as they moved from the initial idea that struck them as worthy of deeper thought to their refined piece of writing, ready for national publication. Teaching within school reform provided a cohesive theme for this work.

Using the CES and AISR professional development mailing lists, we invited potential writers from around the country.

> Candidates were sent along by principals like mine, who hoped to get articles written about their schools [that] could be used for publicity and reform. (*Jon Appleby*)

> Our Dean of Faculty handed me the invitation, commenting that she knew I liked to write and thought I would enjoy this work. Her recognition carried me for a few days—to be replaced by the enormous fear of being in the company of *real* writers, where I would be revealed as a fraud. (*Peggy Silva*)

> I had just been talking about starting a writers' group in our English Department meeting on one of our fall professional development days. As we exited the meeting to go to lunch, Nancy dragged me over to Betsy, one of her colleagues in the Special Education Department, convinced she'd be interested in joining us in starting a group. Betsy excitedly started digging in

her voluminous pocketbook as she spoke with us. "Well then here, JoAnne," she said excitedly, pulling an envelope from the bag. "Maybe you'll want to go to this." It was the letter about the writers' conference. It was the letter that changed my life as a teacher and writer from that point forward. (*JoAnne Dowd*)

The invitation to the Writing Within School Reform Retreat was my ticket to a movement for educational change. Writing had never been one of my strengths, but I felt that I had something to say and the conference provided the opportunity for me to say it. I rented a laptop. (*Jan Grant*)

Even as we launched the CES/AISR Writers' Retreats, Joe and I did not know the power that participants would unleash. Why did practitioners come? Perhaps they saw an opportunity to explore their passions—the frustrations and joys, the dilemmas and breakthroughs, the roadblocks and possibilities—as they worked within the realities of daily life in school and lived with a vision of what might be.

We did know—from Joe's work with the Boston Writing Project and mine as a secondary school teacher of writing—about the fragile wings of fledgling writers. In order for teachers to write for an audience they needed time away from the classroom, specific writing time, sharing and listening time, and a nurturing environment. Each conference began on a Thursday with a welcoming dinner and a writing session.

I remember the food! As a public school teacher, I was not used to being treated as an honored guest at a banquet, but that's what this was. One session began in a conference center at Brown University, and we were served fresh salmon. Isn't it interesting that I remember that meal so clearly? I felt pampered, and knew I wanted to meet Grace and Joe's expectations. (*Peggy Silva*)

Participants—elementary, middle, and high school teachers and principals—had put in a full day by the time they arrived to work with us. Many had come alone from places like San Diego and Hawaii—on red-eye flights—and from Chicago, Bangor, Maine, and

Kingston, RI. While a few had already written for publication, most had not.

> When I heard the sophisticated conversations around me, I became terrified. People were talking about their latest published book, for God's sake! Questions tumbled through my mind: What on earth am I doing here? Is this a challenge certain to end in failure? What shall I say? What will I write? Why did I come? (*Jan Grant*)

As participants finished dessert, Joe "remembered" out loud. He told a story about his stunning discovery, in his 40s, that his father could read and write Slovak. Joe was working with bilingual classrooms at the time, and suddenly realized his own personal connection to bilingual literacy. The purpose of the storytelling was to set the groundwork for reflection and writing in the "I remember" writing activity mentioned in Figure 11.2. When Joe finished his story, he asked practitioners to take 2 minutes to list their own "I remembers" about their own learning. Then he gave clear directions about sharing. "Let's go around the room to share. Just read one 'I remember' without introduction or comment." After the reading, he said, "Take ninety seconds to add to your list." Charged by hearing what others had said, participants wrote.

> I had to remove myself from the crowded dinner table to write. I sat on the floor of that fancy hotel in my schoolmarm dress. We had been issued those composition books with the black and white swirly covers. I just started writing and couldn't stop, even when Joe called "time" on us. I just kept remembering things—a flood of memories, good and bad, happy and tragic. I sat there on the floor with tears streaming down my face and dripping onto the page, but I just couldn't stop writing. I must have filled twenty pages in that first few minutes of frantic release. (*JoAnne Dowd*)

As part of the writing process, participants then circled three statements they wanted to think more about. For each of these sentences they developed a paragraph, then they chose one of those paragraphs to share with a partner. The room was alive with the

---

Figure 11.2
"I Remember" Writing Activity

Facilitator "remembers" aloud something about a personal learning experience. The facilitator tells the story behind the event to give participants an opportunity to settle in and make connections between memories and practice. The facilitator leading the process says:

1. Take 2 minutes to write a list of "I remember . . ." about your learning.
2. Let's go around the room to share. Read one "I remember" without introduction or comment.
3. Now take 90 seconds to add to your list.
4. Circle three statements that you want to think more about.
5. Take a total of 10 minutes to write a paragraph about each sentence.
6. Choose one paragraph to share with a partner.
7. Sit alone for 10 more minutes to expand one of your writings.

---

buzz of people in the process of growing into more deeply reflective individuals who would go public with their work.

> I wrote about my grandmother. Joe's memories had triggered an enormous reserve of images for me, and I had tears in my eyes as I wrote. Later on in the school year, our faculty had an art show of sorts, and I proudly placed my writing piece next to the pottery and watercolors on display. (*Peggy Silva*)

To conclude the session, writers sat alone for 10 minutes to expand their writings. By 9:00, they were weary, but each had written and each had shared aloud. They had survived and overcome the anxiety of entering what had felt like a high-risk experience.

For the first conference two published writers joined us as guest facilitators and models. Each had written from experience in education. Kathleen Cushman, writer/editor of *Horace*, a monthly CES publication, wrote regularly about other practitioners; Mike Rose, author of *Lives on the Boundary* (and currently, *Working Life*) used his own life and teaching practice as the narrative thread that connected his ideas about working with disadvantaged learners.

Both Kathleen and Mike led sessions. Kathleen, for example, led a session on creating images. She read from a text, then asked participants to create their own images. She said: "Take 20 minutes. Find an image. Show it to us. Don't try to tell us what it means or interpret it in any way. Just bring the image to life."

> Twenty minutes? I can't do this. It takes me hours to figure out what I want to write about. What am I doing here, anyway? With the fear of being found out, I carried my computer off to a corner to begin. Somehow, as I called up a blank document to the screen, Meghan, my most troubled student, appeared in my mind. I wrote:
>
> > Meghan rarely walks through the hallways—she skips. Short even for a fourth grader, her head rises and falls through the crowd of classmates, her impish smile appearing and disappearing, her poorly cut dark hair dancing to the tune of her skips. If I'm close enough to her, I can see a light in her eyes, a sparkle, a rainbow radiating all the promise that should rightfully be in the face of an eight-year-old.
> >
> > She's a different person when she isn't skipping. Her head hangs low, usually tilted slightly to one side, eyes on the floor. The smile is gone, the spark extinguished from her eyes. The feet shuffle through the motions of taking her from one place to another, the weight of her world so nearly visible on her small shoulders that she seems to shrink.
>
> Kathleen called us back to the circle and asked us to read around. I was near the end, and so, nervous about how my piece would be received, I recall little of what else was read, except that so many of the others had written pages in the time it had taken me to write two short paragraphs. When my turn came, I held my voice still and read.
>
> Kathleen's response, though short, kept me in the room. "Nice. I think I know Meghan." (*Simon Hole*)

Later, Mike Rose asked participants to talk about their writing lives, those lives that most had never considered or talked about, particularly in connection with their professional lives. They talked. He listened.

Deborah Meier, founder of Central Park East Elementary and Secondary Schools in New York City, was writing her first book at the time. She had almost finished *The Power of Their Ideas,* but she was having trouble with the first chapter. So she had joined us as a participant.

> Debbie Meier and Mike Rose were authors—of books! What was I doing here? And what were they doing listening to me as if I too were a writer? Looking back, I think I felt bullied into writing. When Grace and Joe asked us to list our plans for writing, I remember talking about gathering first-person narratives from my colleagues and my students about our experiences in starting a school. Mike Rose nodded, and offered concrete suggestions—as if I were actually going to do what I said. Grace expected me to. And so I did. It was that simple, and that complicated.
>
> Grace kept in contact with me and offered me another writers' retreat—if I had a draft of a work-in-process. I wrote a draft, I think, to pretend I was a writer so that I could attend another writing conference. Grace's belief in me came before my own belief in myself. (*Peggy Silva*)

Doubts. Fears. Validation. Support. All of these were part of the process of experiencing what it means to learn among colleagues.

The following year Joe and I began with a new group. This second writers' retreat was partially funded by the National Science Foundation. Some participants from the first year attended and facilitated small group feedback sessions. Since half the participants were math or science teachers, we invited as guest facilitator an eminent scientist who had written for a general audience. Sylvia Earle used her newly published *Sea Change* as the basis for her work with the group. With her we created this writing prompt: "Write about a time when you encountered a critter."

> I remember Sylvia Earle coming and sitting on the floor with a small group of us who had shunned the furniture and our

shoes. She did the same. She hunkered down with us, this amazing courageous very public woman, and worked with us as a peer, a colleague, an equal. We shared animal anecdotes from our writing prompt. She shared equally from hers as we did ours. I remember her talking about what it was like to swim with a whale for the first time. I remember her genuine enthusiasm and encouragement for other people's stories of far less exotic experiences with animals like squirrels and mice. (*JoAnne Dowd*)

The prompt was fun. We laughed at snake, turtle, squirrel, and mice stories. As we listened to critter encounters, read aloud, it became evident that these stories would become metaphors for changing practice. We were digging deeper.

Participants had short blocks of time for writing. In small peer editing groups they asked questions about their own writing and their practice. They heard and utilized feedback on their works-in-progress, and they responded to the work of others in meaningful ways using the protocol for peer editing listed in Figure 11.3.

I remember having pastel-colored protocol sheets—structured guides—that we all followed religiously, afraid of offending our fellow fledgling writers, hoping they could hear what we had to say, trying to find a voice, not only in the written word that could be heard but also in the spoken word that could be heard by the new authors. (*JoAnne Dowd*)

Sitting in the lounge of Thayer Street Quad at Brown, I experienced direct peer feedback on my writing, and by indirection on my teaching, for the first time. I was stunned and elated. That experience prefigured and prepared me for coaching a Critical Friends Group and for thinking better, alone and with others, about my work as a teacher. (*Jon Appleby*)

By Saturday, most participants had begun a single piece to work on during the following year. They formed peer support groups for the long haul. By staying with the same writing for a year, they would not only hone and polish it for publication, but they would also delve into every sentence, phrase, and word that spoke about their teaching.

Figure 11.3
Protocol for Peer Editing

Each group of three should have a copy of the writing. Each should have read it before coming to the session, but may need to look it over. Groups assign a timekeeper and a facilitor.

1. Members of the group introduce themselves as writers. What work does each have in progress? What challenges are they facing with the work-in-progress? (10 minutes)
2. Individual writers talk about their work-in-progress that is being presented for the group's assistance. What stage of development do they perceive the work to be in? What are the strengths of the work? Where do they need help? What kind of feedback would they like? (10 minutes)
3. Peer editors practice active listening. (They ask questions about the writer's work, rather than telling their own stories.)
4. The two peer editors talk together about the manuscript. The writer "overhears" the conversation, but does not join in. Editors talk specifically about the strengths as they see them. They may raise questions and talk about what they see as possible next steps for revision. Should the writing be split into two or three pieces? Should it be expanded? All of this must be done within the parameters of the kind of feedback requested. (15 minutes)
5. Writer responds to "overheard" conversation followed by a general discussion about the manuscript led by a group facilitator. (20 minutes)
6. This is the time for addressing grammatical problems. *This step should always be done last.*

(Boston Writing Project Response Group Guidelines)

They would ask: Is this what I really mean to say? What does this process mean in terms of my classroom and my students?

On that last morning of the retreat, an editor's panel talked about the realities of publishing in the world at large. A National Public Radio producer/editor, a newspaper reporter/editor, two book editors, and the editor for a periodical spoke and answered questions from aspiring writers. Even though they would write within our safety net of support for a year, they wanted to hear the voices of experience, to know about what lay beyond. The session prompted new questions, such as, What are the political implications of going public with practice?

The question of rejection loomed large, too. Editors said that timing and "fit" to the occasion or publication were key factors in the acceptance/rejection decisions, not some notion of pure quality—Is it good enough? Am I a good enough writer?—what novices to the process had assumed would be the central issue.

The initial retreat had been in October, and the first deadline for works-in-progress was in January. We promised that if writers stayed with the process, draft after draft, they would eventually produce a publishable piece. If they could manage the May deadline, their work would be published in the Annenberg Institute for School Reform publication series, called *Writing Within School Reform*. We had no wiggle room. Our fiscal year ended in June.

We formed a developmental editorial board just as we had with *The Teacher's Journal*. This time it was comprised of Joe and me along with four new practitioner editors from our writers' retreats. Our board sat together in January when the first works-in-progress came in.

> I remember thinking that editing was both harder and easier—
> harder, because I felt an intense obligation and need to be fair
> to the writers, and easier because the work was not my own.
> Trying to help others make improvements was part of my own
> developmental process. (*Jon Appleby*)

By springtime it was clear that some writers needed another round of person-to-person contact, so we planned an April retreat. The admission ticket to that retreat was a work-in-progress.

> I loved this, as it put us on truly equal ground. For me this
> was a key transition point from the larger group, which

wanted to talk about writing to the smaller group willing to risk doing it. I was one of two writers participating from my school. I wrote a draft—my ticket—and my colleague didn't. While I liked my colleague and respected him, I wanted to stop talking and do. I was hooked. (*Jon Appleby*)

I remember showing up at the Alton Jones Retreat Center, awed by its natural beauty and ready to work. In a way I felt like a monk in a cell, observing a vow of silence, except for the brief times we came together for meetings. The superintendent, as a sign of support for the kind of work I and others from my school were engaged in, loaned me his laptop computer. (*JoAnne Dowd*)

Alton Jones was a peaceful escape. I got to sit and stare at water for long periods of time. I had a lot on my mind then. I had a very troubled student at school, and no idea how to help him. Although I kept trying to think of topics to write about, I couldn't stop thinking of this boy. Finally, out of respect for the process, I sat down at my computer and wrote of my frustration with my inability to help this child. When I had to share my writing, I apologized to the group by saying that I had to clear this "cobweb" from my mind before I could really write what I wanted to. Their response to that first draft humbled me. They could see that boy and hear my anguish, not by what I said, but by what I wrote. And so, that group helped me to discover how to write. Antoine Saint Exupery said that what is essential is invisible to the eye. That night I learned that what is essential can be made visible through writing. (*Peggy Silva*)

On the first night of the retreat, participants wrote journal entries and shared with the group. The prompt: In what ways have you seen your work, your colleagues, and yourselves differently since the October retreat?

These are samples of what some participants wrote:

When I wrote my monograph piece it changed the way I looked at school and the way I looked at my colleagues. It most profoundly changed the way I looked at my students. It helped me to take my students more seriously as collaborators. (*Jon Appleby*)

The more of this work I do the more simple and direct my comments on student work. I'm writing to the students rather than to their writing. (*JoAnne Dowd*)

After October, I realized that I "publish" every day when I write to students. My life as a writer deepens my practice. I am more aware of what I do because I'm now thinking of my words as communication with my readers—my students. (*Peggy Silva*)

After writing journal entries and sharing, participants told Joe and me what they needed next. Together we constructed an agenda to address those needs.

In addition, throughout the 3 days, Joe and I held individual consultations. I remember knowing that I had to speak with Jon Appleby alone, at length, and waiting for just the right time. Something about the tone of his writing was interfering with his message. It was hard for me to think about what to say to him, how to affirm his writing while suggesting that something significant had to change. I saw his light on and knew he was writing. I screwed up my courage and tapped on his door. Our talk that night about turning inward and writing for ourselves, then turning outward and revising for an audience, formed a basis for the writing group that we still have today—7 years later.

"What worked for you?" we asked participants at the end of the 3-day retreat. They began by thanking us for the one-on-one support. They said that shaping their own agenda gave them an opportunity to write and read at those times most appropriate to their own work habits. They found being on "editorial boards"—on which they reviewed the works of others—was a valuable experience for their work as practitioners back at the workplace. They liked working with protocols—step-by-step guides—for the delicate feedback process. And they enjoyed the problem-solving sessions. At first the problems were technical, then the group uncovered writing problems and issues—focus, responsibility, privacy, politics, despair—which led them to deeper insight into their work both as writers and as practitioners.

"What should we do differently another time?" we asked. The conversation was about computer programs, about computer availability, and about having enough copies of each work for editorial boards. But they also wished that they could extend the process of writing with support to their daily life in schools.

Participants said that writing about their own practice for publication changed their professional lives.

I became a better teacher. I began to share my writing with my kids. (*Jon Appleby*)

My colleague Edorah Frazer and I had documented our work on examining my professional portfolio for career advancement in our high school. What had started out as a joyful writing idea became a painful experience. Grace hung in there with us, encouraging us to keep writing. She helped us discover the courage to open our work to an audience; in doing so, we provoked our colleagues to examine our portfolio process, and we entered a national conversation about helping teachers to learn about themselves and their practice. Without a strong mentor, we would have abandoned the writing, and if we had abandoned the writing, Edorah and I would have abandoned our friendship. The writing provided a bridge between experience and dialogue. (*Peggy Silva*)

Writing about my experiences in the classroom allows me to engage with my students on a lot of new levels. For one, seeing myself as a "writer" allows me a new legitimacy when teaching the writing process. I share pieces of my work with students and tell them that I am writing about them. I include their voices in my work and am currently coauthoring a piece with a student. It certainly makes for much more authentic classroom conversations about the writing process. In addition, by writing about incidents that have powerfully affected me, I can "offer up" my learning to others and look for universal themes and ideas. On a more personal level, writing about the experiences allows me to digest them better and make sense of them for myself. (*JoAnne Dowd*)

Not all those who began the process with Joe and me made their work public in the same way. (See Figure 11.4 for a description of the process for creating a catalyst for reflective practice.) After receiving a year of support, some did not publish their writings about their changing practice in a publication issued by CES, AISR, or EDC. With the confidence that comes with experience, I can say, however, that no one fell by the proverbial wayside. Attendance at a retreat or workshop—going public with writing—impacts the individual. Writing is a reflective process. All participants wrote about practice, shared their writing, and received feedback on it—and by extension on their interpretation of their own practice. All participants carried the experience with them when they returned to the arena of teaching and learning with students.

In 1996 I left AISR to return to the classroom. During this time Education Development Corporation (EDC) picked up the work with practitioner writers for a year. With EDC as our sponsor, Joe and I worked as consultants with guest facilitator Bill Ayers, editor of *A Simple Justice: The Challenge of Small Schools*, and a new group of aspiring writers in education.

Meanwhile, a core group of CES and AISR writers, now colleagues and friends, felt the need to continue our work together. Some of us still work as consultants for AISR. We seize the opportunity to meet—at least four times a year—in Boston, Philadelphia, or wherever we find ourselves, and we bring our writing.

> Moving across the country and missing two major meetings of the group gave me a deep sense of personal loss. The work we are doing is so important to me on so many levels, and having been a member of the "founding group," I felt frustrated and bereft to miss even one important conversation the group was having. We own the work that much. (*JoAnne Dowd*)

Now—over 8 years after the first writers' retreat—we call ourselves Educators Writing for Change (EWC). As I write on a foggy morning, I wait for the arrival of a dozen guests for 3 days—old writing friends and new. We come to the group—independently and unfunded—to play with a new idea, to request feedback on a work in progress, and to offer reader response to others. We also come to redefine ourselves as professionals, both individually and as a group.

Figure 11.4
A Catalyst for Reflective Practice

A process for creating a group whose purpose is to write for publication as a way into reflective practice.

1. Plan an opening "thinking about practice and writing for publication" retreat of 2 nights and 2 days (Thursday night through Saturday). Include in the plan support for over a year's time for participants to grow as reflective practitioners and writers for publication. This plan must also include editorial support and publication opportunities at the conclusion of the yearlong process.
2. Gather a group of educators willing to think and write about practice (for a group of 25 or 30, you will need two facilitators).
3. Begin on the first evening with dinner and after-dinner writing prompts, followed by writing and sharing—as a catalyst and entry point for going public with writing.
4. Over 2 days, create opportunities for writers to write and receive feedback on numerous short pieces, from which each will choose one that will lead back into practice and develop as a piece of writing over time.
5. Form peer support groups for the year.
6. Set interim dates for draft submission.
7. Create a developmental editorial board from the group of practitioners to critique writings and assist writers.
8. Offer a second gathering to deepen understanding of both the process of writing and the teaching practice from which the writing springs. A draft of an article is the ticket to the second gathering.

We have grown in our thinking—as practicing educators—about what writing means in our own professional lives and about how it can be a vehicle for better education. Through writing we can share our thinking with others in a way that would otherwise be impossible. With EWC editorial and collegial support, individuals have published widely in educational journals. Some of us are now targeting mainstream publications. Together, we have published *The School Unseen,* our own collection of writings focused on students (see www. members.tripod.com/Simon_Hole/index.html, or e-mail Grace Hall McEntee *gmcente@aol.com* for a hard copy). These writings, intended for a public audience, explore issues not ordinarily raised outside the walls of school and classrooms.

We provide roundtables using these writings from *The School Unseen* to share practitioner thinking—our thinking—with others. We believe that educator writers do change their own practice and can change the way schools, classrooms, and kids are seen. Because we so strongly believe, we have dedicated ourselves to continue supporting each other and to release new practitioner writers.

> I often puzzle over the question of why so many teachers don't write. I suspect it's because the culture among adults in our schools doesn't allow us to be nurturing. (*Jon Appleby*)

> With encouragement, I keep writing because I do believe that I have something to say. (*Jan Grant*)

> When I began to write, I found myself trying to understand the "story" of my teaching. What are the themes that run through it? Where are the conflicts and how do I find resolution? Writing about teaching truly is reflective practice. In addition, I find myself better able to understand the struggles that my students are involved in around writing and I'm probably more appreciative of their products. (*Steve Dreher*)

REFERENCES

Ayers, W., Klonsky, M., & Lyon, G. H. (Eds.). (2000). *A simple justice: The challenge of small schools.* New York: Teachers College Press.

Earle, S. (1995). *Sea change: A message of the oceans.* New York: G. P. Putnam's Sons.

Meier, D. (1995). *The power of their ideas: Lessons for America from a small school in Harlem.* Boston: Beacon Press.

Rose, M. (1989). *Lives on the boundary: A moving account of the struggles and achievements of America's educationally unprepared.* New York: Penguin Books.

Rose, M. (forthcoming). *Working lives.* New York: Viking/Penguin.

Index

About the Authors

Educators Writing for Change is a group of educators convinced that their voices have something to add to the national dialogue concerning the rethinking of public schooling. Originally brought together by Grace Hall McEntee and Joseph Check for a project funded by the Coalition of Essential Schools and the Annenberg Institute for School Reform at Brown University, they meet several times a year to share their writing. As they have spent considerable time within public school classrooms—a total of 123 years—their writing has focused on telling the stories of life within schools and on their own changing practice.

Jon Appleby teaches English to juniors and seniors at Noble High School in North Berwick, Maine. A graduate of Wesleyan University with a Master's in Education from the University of Southern Maine, he has taught alternative classes, adult education, and electives in writing and philosophy. Jon Appleby can be reached at joldappleby@aol.com.

Joseph W. Check has been working with practitioner writers for more than twenty years. He is Director of the Leadership in Urban Schools Doctoral Program and of the Boston Writing Project at the University of Massachusetts, Boston. His most recent book is *Politics, Language, and Culture: A Critical Look at Urban School Reform* (2002).

JoAnne Dowd is the curriculum coordinator for School Administrative Unit 21 in Hampton, New Hampshire, working with several seacoast schools. She is a Critical Friends coach and national CFG trainer of coaches. A graduate of University of New Hampshire with an M.A.T. in English Teaching, JoAnne taught grades 7–12 in rural Maine for 12 years. She is currently researching the link between access to resources and student achievement, as well as the effect of data-based decision making on school reform efforts. JoAnne Dowd's e-mail address is Maddogdowd64@hotmail.com.

Jan Grant is the founder and director of Forum and Associates, a consulting firm in Kingston, Rhode Island, dedicated to educational reform initiatives. Her K–12 teaching experience in history, English, social studies, and theater resulted in her current passion—the study and research of process education in nonjudgmental learning environments. Jan is a member of the National School Reform Faculty and a Coach of Critical Friends Groups for students, teachers, administrators, and superintendents. Jan Grant can be reached at grantj@ride.ri.net.

Simon Hole has been teaching fourth grade in Narragansett, Rhode Island, since 1975. His association with the Coalition of Essential Schools and the National Re:Learning Faculty has led him to question nearly every aspect of his teaching practice. He is currently conducting research into the thinking processes used by proficient problem solvers. Simon Hole's e-mail address is ropajavi@aol.com.

Grace Hall McEntee was a teacher of students for 24 years in public secondary schools, where she also served as Department Head of English and Brown University Coordinator for student teachers at the Toll Gate Complex in Warwick, Rhode Island. For 4 years she worked as a senior associate for professional development at Brown University, coaching teachers for the Coalition of Essential Schools and the Annenberg Institute for School Reform (AISR). She was cofounder and editor of the AISR Writing Within School Reform Publication Series and cofounder of a nonprofit group called Educators Writing for Change. Grace received a Master of Arts degree in English from the University of Rhode Island. She has studied writing at Fairfield University, Bard College, Iowa Writers' Festival, and Harvard University Extension School. She is now a writer, consultant, and student of herbal healing. Grace Hall McEntee's e-mail address is gmcente@aol.com.

Peggy Silva, a charter member of the faculty of Souhegan High School in Amherst, New Hampshire, is currently the coordinator of Souhegan's writing center. For the first 10 years of the school, she taught ninth-grade humanities as a member of a heterogeneous, interdisciplinary team. Peggy serves as a facilitator for the National School Reform Faculty (NSRF), as a Coach of a Critical Friends Group, and as a supervisor for the University of New Hampshire's graduate intern program. She is the coauthor of *Standards of Mind and Heart: Creating the Good High School*, published by Teachers College Press in 2002. Peggy's e-mail addresses are peggysilva1@earthlink.net and PSilva@sprise.com.